From the Workers' State to the Golden State

THE NEW IMMIGRANTS SERIES

Allyn & Bacon

Series Editor, Nancy Foner, State University of New York at Purchase

From the Workers' State to the Golden State:

Jews from the Former Soviet Union in California

Steven J. Gold
Michigan State University

Allyn and Bacon
Boston • London • Toronto • Sydney • Tokyo • Singapore

For Lisa

Copyright © 1995 by Allyn and Bacon
A Division of Simon and Schuster
160 Gould Street
Needham Heights, Massachusetts 02194

ISBN: 0-205-16702-0

Printed in the United States of America

10 9 8 7 6 5 4 3 2 1   99 98 97 96 95

Contents

Foreword to the Series

The United States is now experiencing the largest wave of immigration in the country's history. The 1990s, it is predicted, will see more new immigrants enter the United States than in any decade in American history. New immigrants from Asia, Latin America, and the Caribbean are changing the American ethnic landscape.

Until recently, immigration was associated in the minds of many Americans with the massive influx of southern and eastern Europeans at the turn of the century. Since the late 1960s, America has again become a country of large-scale immigration, this time attracting newcomers from developing societies of the world. The number of foreign-born is at an all-time high: nearly 20 million foreign-born persons were counted in the 1990 census. Although immigrants are a smaller share of the nation's population than they were earlier in the century—8 percent in 1990 compared to about 15 percent in 1910—recent immigrants are having an especially dramatic impact because their geographic concentration is greater today. About half of all immigrants entering the United States during the 1980s moved to eight urban areas: Los Angeles, New York, Miami, Anaheim, Chicago, Washington, D.C., Houston, and San Francisco. America's major urban centers are, increasingly, immigrant cities with new ethnic mixes.

Who are the new immigrants? What are their lives like here? How are they redefining themselves and their cultures? And how are they contributing to a new and changing America? The *New Immigrants Series* provides a set of case studies that explores these themes among a variety of groups. Each book in the series is written by a recognized expert who has done extensive in-depth ethnographic research on one of the immigrant groups. The groups represent a broad range of today's arrivals, coming from a variety of countries and cultures. The studies cover a wide geographical range as well, based on research done in different parts of the country, from New York to California. Most of the books in the series are written by anthropologists. All draw on qualitative research that shows what it means to be an immigrant in America today. As part of each study, individual immigrants tell their stories, which will help give a sense of the experiences and problems of the newcomers. Through the case studies, a dynamic picture emerges of the way immigrants are carving out new lives for themselves at the same time as they are creating a new and more diverse America.

The ethnographic case study, long the anthropologist's trademark, provides a depth often lacking in research on immigrants in the United States. Many anthropologists, moreover, like a number of authors in the *New Immigrants Series*, have done research in the sending society as well as in the United States. Having field experience at both ends of the migration chain makes anthropologists particularly sensitive to the role of transnational ties that link immigrants to their home societies. With first-hand experience of immigrants in their home culture, anthropologists are also well positioned to appreciate continuities as well as changes in the immigrant setting.

As the United States faces a growing backlash against immigration, and many Americans express ambivalence and sometimes hostility toward the latest arrivals, it becomes more important than ever to learn about the new immigrants and to hear their voices. The case studies in the *New Immigrants Series* will help readers understand the cultures and lives of the newest Americans and bring out the complex ways the newcomers are coming to terms with and creatively adapting to life in a new land.

NANCY FONER
Series Editor

INTRODUCTION

THE CHABAD RUSSIAN DAY CAMP

Santa Monica Boulevard is one of the long streets in Los Angeles that runs between downtown and the ocean. The center of LA's Russian emigre community is located on a section of the Boulevard in West Hollywood between the small theaters that are LA's equivalent of New York's "Off Broadway" and the trendy restaurants and condos that attract young celebrities.

Russian emigres live off the main boulevard in two story, stucco apartments and small, Spanish-style houses with tree lawns and yards shaded by the neglected foliage of palms, magnolias and birds of paradise. On a typical summer day, Russian families congregate at picnic tables in Plummer Park, chatting, playing dominoes and offering their children and grandchildren treats from plastic grocery bags that they have carried from home. Scruffy pre-teens, with rollerblades and hockey sticks, are shouting at each other in Russian in a nearby parking lot.

And, across the street, lunch is being served to several hundred school-aged Russian children at a religious day camp. Seated at folding tables, blond and brown-haired boys wearing baseball caps, oversized t-shirts, shorts and basketball shoes eat fish sticks and canned corn from paper plates served by college-aged counselors. After their meal, the counselors lead the boys in boisterous songs and competitive cheering.

In addition to the large influx of Latino immigrants into the Los Angeles area, this community of Russian immigrants is also an integral part of the new multicultural and multiethnic Los Angeles. These emigres from the former Soviet Union and their children are different from the native-born white Protestants who dominated LA as recently as the mid 1960s (Davis 1990: 326). They bring with them values, cultural practices and outlooks towards life that sometimes clash with those held by most native-born Americans. Indeed, the day camp I mentioned is run by Chabad, an ultra-Orthodox Jewish movement considered extreme in its devotion to ancient religious teachings and its rejection of assimilation even by the standards of most American Jews, let alone gentiles. While these baseball cap-wearing, English speaking children seem to be rapidly adopting the folkways of American life, their Russian-born parents, and especially, grandparents often remain passionately attached to the nation they fled as refugees. So much so, that in a community which normally abhors organizations, Soviet Jews have created several veterans associations where elderly emigres celebrate their service in the Red Army.

SOVIET JEWS AS CONTEMPORARY IMMIGRANTS

After three decades of emigration, there are now sizable communities of Jews from the former USSR in several nations and three continents, including Western Europe, North America and Israel (Tress 1994). While the greatest number reside in Israel, since the mid 1960s over 300,000 Jews from the former Soviet Union have settled in the United States (HIAS 1995). Further, from 1988 to the present, persons from the former Soviet Union have been the largest refugee nationality to enter the United States (Littman 1993).

Despite their numbers, relatively little attention or scholarship has addressed the fate of this group. Moreover, with a few important exceptions, in-depth information on Soviet Jews' experience in the U.S., like that on most immigrant groups, has consisted largely of bare bones statistical accounts dealing with age distribution, income and welfare dependency, occupational adjustment and sometimes, religious participation. Even less has been written about these newcomers' style of adaptation and, community formation, ideological outlook, family patterns and adjustment strategies. To fill the void, this book considers the communal and social aspects of Soviet Jewish emigres as they build lives in California.

Soviet Jews: A Unique Group

As recent immigrants to the United States, Jews from the former Soviet Union have a lot of company. During the years when nearly all 325,000 Soviet Jews entered the U.S. (from 1968 to 1993) almost 16 million immigrants came to the U.S. (INS 1993: Table 1). All new immigrants, Soviet Jews included, share common experiences as they adjust to the United States. Soviet Jews in Los Angeles, Dominicans in New York, and Pakistanis in Chicago must find work, learn English, adapt previous family patterns, develop social networks, and generally establish an acceptable way of life in a strange new environment.

However, each group's experience is also unique. Because of their social characteristics, their origins in the former Soviet Union, and their patterns of resettlement, many features typical to Soviet Jews contrast dramatically with those of other contemporary immigrant nationalities.

Much of the Soviet Jews' uniqueness can be traced to their origins in the Soviet Union, which, until its recent downfall, was the oldest and most highly developed communist nation on earth. A notable characteristic of communist societies is the fact that almost every aspect of life—from the production of butter and the administration of summer camps to the shaping of ideology—is under government control. Because the Soviet system functioned for more than six decades, its citizens were totally immersed in this system for generations.

As a result of their communist background, Soviet Jews bring a set of expectations and outlooks that mark them off from other migrant communities. Most migrants come from nations which offer fewer services to their citizens than does the United States; they do not generally expect government agencies to provide them with jobs, housing, day care or other basic needs. In contrast, Jews from the former Soviet Union come from a country where virtually all of life's basic necessities were delivered by the government. In adjusting to life in America, these refugees must unlearn a whole set of techniques associated with securing what they require from bureaucracies. Emigres must discover new ways of filling needs as they combine resources available in America's free market economy and limited welfare state and make use of charitable social agencies and personal or community arrangements.

Because of the Soviet government's involvement in nearly all aspects of social and political life, emigres are not accustomed to the many freedoms that Americans, and many other immigrants, take for granted. Even such mundane possibilities as opening a business, practicing one's religion, running for office, starting a newspaper, carrying a protest sign or forming a political club were restricted prior to the Soviet Union's demise.

As white Europeans, Soviet Jews are members of the racial majority group in the United States. This is not true for most new immigrants, who are from Asia, Latin America and the Caribbean. Coming to the United States means a painful encounter with prejudice and discrimination for nonwhite newcomers. Not so for Jews from the former USSR. Indeed, they leave minority status behind when they come to this country. In this way, they also differ from white immigrants from places like Canada or Scotland who belonged to the dominant group in their home nation as well in the U.S.

Russian Jews have suffered centuries of discrimination, violence, and oppression in eastern Europe, where they have been so "beyond the veil" of social acceptance that historian John Hope Franklin likened their condition to the status of Blacks in the old South (Franklin 1992: 17). Only fifty years ago, six million people—including old women and babies—were annihilated in Eastern Europe simply because they were Jews.

Russian Jews find themselves to be much closer to the racial mainstream in the U.S. than in their homeland. Admittedly, as foreigners, Jews, and former citizens of "the evil empire," they are distinct from native born Christians in this country. Nevertheless, because they are educated, Caucasian, legal residents who tend to live in cities with large nonwhite and immigrant populations, Russian Jews are among the elite of recent migrant groups in terms of both class and race.

Jews from the former Soviet Union have another advantage that most recent immigrant groups lack: access to established—and prosperous—communities in the U.S. By virtue of their connections to American Jews (who have worked to bring them here), Soviet Jews have well connected sponsors when they arrive. Like other immigrant groups, Soviet Jews are drawn to California for its mild climate, robust economy, high quality public universities, toleration of diverse lifestyles and generous welfare benefits. Since many of these immigrants are engineers, the high concentration of engineering jobs in the region is also an attraction. Another factor is the presence of major Russian speaking and Jewish communities. [California is the primary destination for Soviet Armenian immigrants; Los Angeles has the second largest Jewish community in the U.S., the San Francisco Bay Area, the seventh (ORR 1993; Kosmin and Paretzky 1993)].

While California offers many features that immigrants desire, at the same time, the Golden State also reveals a catalog of modern social problems—crime, pollution, declining public services, a high cost of living—that disturb newcomers. Finally, at least since the economic downturn of the early 1990s, California has been a hotbed of anti-immigrant sentiment, of which Jewish immigrants from the former Soviet Union are keenly aware.

METHODOLOGY

The research reported in this book was collected over a period of about 14 years in both Northern and Southern California. I used participant observation and in-depth interviewing, the same techniques as used in many classic studies of immigrant communities earlier in this century. These methods allowed me to capture a rich and detailed image of the experience of refugees—one with a human face—and to understand immigrants as social actors.

As a research methodology, participant observation offered me several advantages over the statistically-based survey research methods favored by many sociologists. Survey data are generally collected at a single point in time. Respondents fill out questionnaires, which are later analyzed. However, participant observation research takes place over a long period of time—in the case of this study, well over ten years. In this way, I was able to understand the process involved as immigrants settled in the U.S., learned English, got jobs and developed a perspective on their new lives. As I gained knowledge and insight about emigres' experiences, I was able to include it in my on-going analysis by returning to the field where I could verify and refine my interpretations through additional observations of and discussion with members of the community.

Keeping in touch with community's progress, over the years, I was able to maintain contact with many emigre individuals and networks. I took note as the Wiseman children finished school, moved out of their parents' home and had their own kids. I watched the Chabad-Russian synagogue grow from a small storefront operation to a major force in the community. I noted the increasing proliferation of Russian-language signs in West Los Angeles and also observed the closing of the community's most prestigious restaurant near Beverly Hills. I became acquainted with the community's right wing journalists and punk-rock artists. I had regular conversations with emigre students during their four years in college. And as time passed, I saw emigre leaders and organizations rise and fall in community influence.

A further advantage of participant observation is that it allows an observer to learn about *group* life. Because survey questionnaires are normally filled out by a single individual, surveys are not very sensitive to the collective nature of social life. However, by performing participant observation research, one is in a much better position to learn about groups. During fieldwork, I observed emigre families as they ate dinner, talked about politics or watched TV, I looked on at religious services, in ethnic businesses, and at weddings and nightclubs. I was also present while representatives of Soviet Jewish organizations spoke with their resettlement staff. In all of these settings, I could collect information about the collective life and culture of this new immigrant group in a way unlikely to be captured in a written questionnaire.

A final advantage offered by the use of participant observation and open-ended interviews in this study is that it allowed me to develop trusting and personal relationships with my respondents. Soviet Jews, having grown up in a rigid, autocratic and highly controlled society, tend to be very suspicious of bureaucrats, regarding all officials in much the same way that Americans view IRS agents. Moreover, as refugees, they are quite wary of those who they feel might intend to manipulate or harm them. Because of this, they place little value in institutionally-based relationships. In contrast, however, Soviet Jews are often warm, hospitable and personable people who place great moral value in social relationships. If I had used survey questionnaires to study emigres, they would have likely seen these as some form of bureaucratic prying into their lives and given little attention to their responses—perhaps even distorting answers on purpose. However, by collecting data about emigres in the context of a face to face conversation (with my initial contact generally established through a referral from one of their trusted friends), I could reduce emigres' fears and suspicions and relate to them in the personal manner. In these several ways, I believe that the qualitative research methods I chose for this study were especially appropriate and allowed me to collect rich and meaningful responses.

I began my research by taking a volunteer position as an English tutor. In this capacity, I made weekly visits to the home of a Soviet Jewish family in San Francisco for 15 months. As time passed, we became friendly and introduced each other to our friends and relatives in the local community. I became familiar with a broad network of refugees ranging from college students, young couples with American-born children, and elderly migrants who knew only a few words of English.

To learn about the resettlement system and its clients, I served for two years as a resettlement worker, first as a volunteer and later for pay, in two San Francisco resettlement agencies. I also taught a job-finding class for Soviet emigres at the Oakland Jewish Community Center and became a member of several immigrant-service committees of the Los Angeles Jewish Federation. By participating in academic conferences on Soviet Jewish adjustment to the U.S., I was able to meet a number of emigre scholars and community leaders who themselves were involved in research on various aspects of their group's experience. Finally, as a professor, I encountered and worked with several emigre undergraduate and graduate students. Their comments and insights helped me to understand the experience of adolescent refugees.

These settings offered several opportunities to gain a detailed view of Soviet Jewish refugees' experience. I attended numerous refugee community events, spent time in refugee neighborhoods and attended religious services at Russian Jewish synagogues. As I performed volunteer work on behalf of refugees, I was also able to see how they dealt with problems of adjustment to American society. Since field work and interviewing took place in refugees' homes, resettlement agencies, businesses, synagogues, and neighborhoods, I collected most of my data on immigrants' own turf.

In order to meet a broader section of the refugee community, I also conducted in-depth interviews with 68 refugees and 25 non-refugee service providers. Interviews, which were conducted in English, ranged from half-an-hour to several hours weekly over the course of a year and a half. Quotes used throughout the book, are taken directly from interview transcripts. In order to insure confidentiality, respondents' names are pseudonyms.

I identified interview subjects with the aid of snowball sample referrals which meant that the people I interviewed referred me to additional respondents from their social networks. Also, I found respondents through ethnic publications, listings in the telephone directory and lists made available to me by resettlement agencies and refugee organizations. I made specific efforts to observe and interview refugees representing a wide variety of social categories. These included political activists, religious leaders, resettlement workers, business owners and college students, men and women, the young and the old, the well settled and the recently arrived, and those in middle class and working class occupations. Although I did research in both the San Francisco Bay Area and Los Angeles, I also visited Soviet Jewish communities in Cleveland, New York and Boston to get a greater sense of the emigre experience in a variety of settings.

While this is a qualitative study, at times I refer to statistical information about Jews from the former Soviet Union as collected in a variety of community-based and national surveys.[1] In the end, through a variety of research techniques, I have been able to paint a broad portrait of the Soviet Jewish population that highlights the diversity and processes that constitute central themes of recent immigrant life.

---

1. For extensive statistical data on Jews from the former Soviet Union in the U.S., see (Gold 1994)

Acknowledgments

Support for the completion of this book was provided by the John Randolph Haynes and Dora Haynes Foundation, the University of California at Berkeley Regents Fellowship and Chancellors Patent Fund, the U.S. Department of Labor, International Division and Michigan State University. Interview tapes were carefully transcribed by Sheila Jones, Sharon Reina and Cynthia Hutchinson.

Vladimir Schlapentokh, Bruce Phillips, Roger Waldinger, Madeleine Tress, David Haines, Fran Markowitz, Yoav Ben-Horin, Mia Tuan and Ruth Seldin gave valuable comments and materials. Sylvia Shepard offered many insightful suggestions for planning and organizing the book. Nancy Foner provided guidance as well as very detailed comments on many aspects of the book.

Lisa Gold copy edited the text, and along with William and Betty Gold offered their unyielding support and encouragement for the project.

Finally, I wish to thank all of the respondents who cooperated with the research. Although they remain anonymous, the study would not have been possible without them. All of those mentioned above have generously contributed to the study. Any errors within it, however, are my responsibility alone.

WHY DID THEY COME?

Background, Migration Experience and Social Characteristics

WHO ARE THE SOVIET JEWS?

The nearly 325,000 Jews from the former Soviet Union who have settled in the United States since the mid 1960s have arrived in two distinct flows. The first group, who entered from about 1972 to 1986, came as refugees from a functioning and highly restrictive communist nation. Since about 1986—the beginning of the glasnost era—thousands more have exited a society marked by increases in both freedom and social disorganization. (Glasnost refers to the policy of openness in the Soviet Union introduced by Prime Minister Mikhail Gorbachev. During this time, many of the strict regulations which had been maintained from the time of the Revolution in 1917 were relaxed).

Although they come from the former Soviet Union, the new arrivals are of course Jews. What this means is a complex question. Being Jewish involves both religion and ethnicity. Many Jews in America practice the Jewish religion. In this way, they are like other religious denominations in American society such as Methodists, Catholics, and Hindus. However, a considerable part of the community—known as ethnic or

1

secular Jews—are largely ignorant of theology and follow few religious rituals. In American society, the group membership of secular Jews is similar to that of national origin groups. Like Italians, Chinese or Dominicans, Jews may speak a certain language, eat distinctive foods, celebrate specific holidays, and listen to types of music associated with "the old country." Also, like various nationality groups, they are associated with particular neighborhoods, occupations, and political views and convey gestures, patterns of speech and physical traits that make them readily identifiable.

However, unlike most nationality groups, Jews come from a variety of national origins in Europe, the Americas, North Africa and the Middle East and generally embody many of the characteristics of the countries in which they lived: North African Jews speak Arabic, eat couscous, are soccer fans, and at least to many Westerners, look "North African." Likewise, except for their religious orientation and perhaps their surnames, British Jews are virtually indistinguishable from non-Jewish Britons. Hence, Judaism has religious, ethnic, and national dimensions. Jews from the former Soviet Union are one of these many Jewish nationality groups. Most are not religious: they are secular Jews. And in terms of culture, language, and nationality, they are Russian.

The new Soviet Jewish immigrants are the latest wave of European Jews to enter the U.S. European Jews have been migrating to this country since the 1600s and over two million arrived in the last great immigration at the turn of the century (Glazer and Moynihan 1963). In many ways, Soviet Jews stand out from earlier waves of Jewish immigrants. They have high levels of education, have lived under communism for generations, and receive many resettlement services when they arrive. Unlike most American Jews, they have had minimal exposure to formal Jewish training and Jewish religious life and no experience with a highly organized Jewish community.

What is a Refugee?

Soviet Jews who have come to the U.S. since the 1960s are also bearers of a particular political status: they are refugees. Governments, the U.S. government among them, classify migrant groups into specific categories associated with various rights and duties. These include permanent residents (voluntary immigrants) who can work and, after five years, apply for citizenship; tourists and students, who are expected to leave the U.S. following a specified interval; and persons with no legal status, who if caught, are subject to deportation. Nearly all Soviet Jews have entered the U.S. within the "refugee" category, which refers to people who leave their country of origin due to a "well founded fear of persecution" for religious, ethnic, political or family reasons (Reimers 1985).

Compared to other legal categories for new arrivals, refugee status is among the most privileged. Refugees receive permanent residency status, the right to work in the U.S., and are eligible for public assistance and a variety of resettlement services. Immigrants, including those with impressive credentials, may have to wait years to enter the U.S. and even then are not entitled to government benefits. Soviet Jews receive this special status because of their long period of oppression in Eastern Europe.

A BRIEF HISTORY OF JEWS IN EASTERN EUROPE AND THE SOVIET UNION

Jews have resided in regions of Eastern Europe and the former Soviet Union for hundreds of years. From the time of the tzars, through the pogroms in the 1880s, to Stalin's purges and the Nazi invasion, and up until the recent era of coerced assimilation without full acceptance, they have been persecuted, massacred, marginalized, and driven out. Nevertheless, Russian Jews have survived. By the 1960s, they were perhaps the most highly educated and urbanized of all nationalities in the USSR. Their rate of membership in the communist party exceeded their representation in the Soviet population (Andreski 1979). Consequently, Soviet Jews have a long and complex history in the USSR and hold mixed feelings towards the country that has provided them with both suffering and opportunity.

The migration of Soviet Jews to the U.S. can be traced to the mid 19th century, when Russia's Jews were restricted to particular geographical regions known as "the pale of settlement" and excluded from all but a few fields of economic endeavor (Zenner 1983; Bonacich 1973; Goldscheider and Zuckerman 1984). Denied citizenship until 1917, they were isolated from the collective allegiances of trust and mutual obligation that made up the social fabric of feudal Russian society. As visible outsiders, they offered an easy scapegoat for native elites when local masses became angry. In the 1880s, anti-Jewish sentiments reached a boiling point, leading to pogroms (government sanctioned, anti-Jewish riots), life-long conscription, and various anti-Semitic movements. The civil service, the professions, and the academy were closed to Jews, and Jewish students were subject to strict quotas in sectarian schools. The following entry from the 1911 *Encyclopedia Britannica* captures Eastern European Jews' situation at the turn of the century: "The congestion within the pale is the cause of terrible destitution and misery. Fierce massacres occurred in Nizhniy-Novgorod in 1882 and in Kishinev in 1903. Many other pogroms have occurred, and the condition of the Jews has been reduced to one of abject poverty and despair." (Abrams 1911: 409). As a result of these unbearable conditions, millions of Jews left Russia for Western Europe and the New World (Jacobs 1981). From 1881 to 1924, 2,338,941 Jews entered the U.S., mostly from Russia (Wirth 1928: 150).

Many of the Jews who remained in Eastern Europe became advocates of the revolution, largely because the communists were the only political group that promised Jews equal rights (Wirth 1928). "Jews played a crucial role in the victory of the Bolsheviks, and it seems likely that without the Jewish brain power their revolution would have failed. . . At the end of Lenin's life most members of the Politburo were Jewish by origin though not, of course, by faith." (Andreski 1979: 153). While the Soviet system seldom gave credit to the role played by Jews in its inception, anti-Communists and ethnic nationalists in the Soviet Union—who have gained strength since the fall of communism—remember and overstate the Jews' role in the revolution to fan the fires of anti-Semitism (Chesler 1974).

Following the revolution, the Communists opposed Jewish religious activities—as well as those of other denominations. However, Yiddish (the German-based, Hebrew-scripted language of Eastern European Jews) and Jewish cultural activities were encouraged until the 1930s. In my interviews, elderly Soviet Jews remembered this idealistic time with fondness, and they credit Soviet reforms with helping their families move out of ghettos and into the professions. While opportunities for educational advancement were open to Soviet Jews from the 1920s until the 1960s, other Stalin-era developments limited their prospects for equal treatment. In order to organize its vast territory, the Soviet government established a policy for dealing with ethnic and national diversity by creating a series of Soviet Republics—Armenia, the Ukraine, Georgia and so on. Although these regions were subject to Soviet hegemony and Russification, they did provide their residents with a measure of autonomy. Jews—whose passports were marked "Jew" as nationality even though most lived in the Russian or Ukrainian Republics—were assigned a homeland in Birobidzhan on the Manchurian boarder, thousands of miles from the European cities where most resided. Few Jews migrated to this Republic. Its existence is seen as an early example of the Soviet system's long-standing efforts to isolate Jews from co-ethnics outside of the USSR (Jacobs 1981: 4).

The USSR also instituted policies to limit Jews' power in the nation's government and bureaucracy. Stalin's reign of purges from the 1920s to the 1950s—the infamous dictator executed or jailed thousands of persons whom he felt threatened his power base—included disproportionate numbers of Jewish victims (Chesler 1974). Between 1937 and 1974, the number of Jewish deputies in the Supreme Soviet was reduced from 47 to 6 (Simon 1985b: 8). "After World War II, Stalin climaxed his anti-Jewish campaigns by arresting and executing the nation's twenty-four leading Yiddish writers" (Orleck 1987:283).

During WWII, many Soviet Jews fled east to escape the advancing Nazis. Most who stayed behind were exterminated. This fact was suppressed by the Soviet government which did not want to admit that Jews suffered more than others.

However, Yevtushenko, the noted Russian man of letters, protested this silence about the Jewish Holocaust in his poem about "Babi Yar," the mass grave for thousands of Ukrainian Jews murdered by the Nazis. Recognition of the victims' religion and the explanation for their annihilation have only been made official since the post-communist era of the late 1980s. Soviet Jews who survived the Nazis contributed heroically to the war effort. Even those who have migrated to the U.S. proudly display their war-time medals at Veterans Day parades, demonstrating an astounding degree of patriotism towards a country which they have just fled as refugees.

Post War activism by Soviet Jews is linked with the formation of Israel. The USSR initially had a positive regard for this nation which upheld many socialist values. However, following the 1967 war, the Soviets took an increasingly dim view of the Jewish State. This was partly due to Soviet efforts to develop good relations with Arab nations. Soviet opposition to Zionism was also based upon a long standing policy of limiting Jews' relations with co-ethnics outside of the USSR.

Many writers suggest that the anti-Zionist articles which appeared with increasing frequency in the Soviet media after 1967 fostered anti-Semitic attacks in the USSR (Jacobs 1981). In my interviews, Soviet emigres claimed that because newspaper articles were approved by the government, Soviet citizens interpreted anti-Zionist polemics as veiled instructions. "Getting the hint," ambitious officials would carry out personal projects of harassing, demoting or refusing to hire Jews as a means of impressing supervisors. Andre, an engineer from Kiev, told me, "It was the same thing as the government saying 'Okay, you can go now guys and freely beat them up.' And that's what happened to me when I was in school—I was beaten up lots of times."

The "lack of nationalism and patriotism" attributed to Jews from the tzarist era continued to be a justification for keeping them from positions of power and influence. After Jews were permitted to emigrate in the 1970s, the same slander also rationalized their exclusion from higher education; the Soviets claimed that they could not invest in the education of persons likely to leave. Such accusations of disloyalty become a self-fulfilling prophesy when Jews, who were denied opportunities within the USSR, were forced to seek them abroad. Prior to the 1960s, the Soviet system offered Jews access to higher education because technical experts were required for the nation's military and industrial development. Soon, however, this path was restricted. "As Khrushchev pointedly indicated, 'we' no longer need the Jews because we have 'our own' experts" (Jacobs 1981:5). After 1967, the number of Jews able to receive a university education was reduced by 50 percent and few if any were admitted to Moscow University, the "Harvard" of the USSR (Simon 1981). In my many interviews, I talked to only one Jew under the age of 35 who was able to obtain higher education in the Ukraine, generally regarded to be the most anti-Semitic Soviet Republic and also the home to almost 800,000 Jews (Simon 1985b: 8). I did interview young Ukrainian Jews with university degrees, but these were obtained outside of their home Republic, sometimes through correspondence schools, which were a common means of acquiring a higher education in the former Soviet Union, although less prestigious than major universities or institutes (Statistical Abstract of the USSR 1979, Vol 80: 492-3).

Jewish Identity by Generation

Soviet political transformations affected the structures of opportunity available to different generations of Jews. The same events also shaped Jews' exposure to and involvement in religion (Orbach 1980; Kochan 1978; Orleck 1987). The elderly are often familiar with traditional East European Judaism that they learned from their parents or in the period before the Stalin-inspired restrictions of the 1930s. In contrast, most middle-aged Soviet Jews grew up in an atheistic environment that encouraged the assimilation of Jews—and other ethnic and nationality groups—to mainstream Soviet/Russian culture. Their experience of Judaism is secular and they tend to have little religious knowledge or sentiment. Andre, an engineer from Kiev who now lives near San Francisco admitted that his family had "no Jewish culture at all . . . we lost it completely. When we went to Vienna, [after leaving the USSR] the resettlement staff looked at our family—we didn't look like Jews to them. And they started to ask questions. What we know about Jewish life? Do we know any holidays? And we were so ashamed. We didn't know any."

Because almost two thirds of Soviet Jews in the U.S. are from the major cities of the Russian and Ukrainian USSR—Moscow, Leningrad (now Saint Petersburg), Odessa, Lvov and Kiev—they were subjected to a national culture intentionally designed by the Soviet government to unify the many ethnic, linguistic and nationality groups in the USSR. The Jews' high levels of education and rates of communist party membership (due to the fact that party membership was required to maximize career opportunities) also fostered assimilation.

In order to escape anti-Semitism and achieve success within Soviet society, many middle aged Soviet Jews actively adopted Russian culture and identity. I interviewed several emigres with Russian or Ukrainian last names who told of a Jewish name in their families' past. Intermarriage with non-Jews was another vehicle for assimilation. In this manner, Jews could change the national affiliation listed on their passport from "Jewish" to "Russian." Assimilationist Jews also chose not to circumcise their sons, even though this meant violating a long-standing Jewish tradition. (In response, emigre synagogues have been active in providing the Bris {ritual circumcision} to Soviet Jewish adults in the U.S.)

As a consequence of their assimilation, the overwhelming majority of Soviet Jews have few distinctly Jewish ethnic or cultural traditions. A report by an emigre activist concluded: "The vehemently anti-religious Soviet system . . . led to the subsequent loss of an individual's identity as a member of the Jewish community" (Terlitsky 1992:14). An exception is the handful of Sephardic Russian Jews hailing from rural regions of the East who have generally resisted modern life and the imposition of Russian language and Soviet culture (Serels 1990).

In fact, the "Jewish" nationality designation on the Soviet passport has probably saved thousands of Soviet Jews from total assimilation into Soviet/Russian society and facilitated their migration to Israel and the West (Gitelman 1992). Despite the trend towards assimilation, several young and middle aged emigres described their continued interest in religious and ethnic activities in the USSR, in part, as a way to express their frustration with the Soviet system or to articulate group identity following the system's collapse. A former linguist, now a Los Angeles social worker, told how he and a group of friends used to meet near the Kiev synagogue because it was "a place for proving to them that we are not afraid, but were proud of being Jews." Another emigre spoke of learning about Jewish holidays with the help of recorded Voice of America radio programs. "We would learn some of the songs. Of course by American standards, they were not great. We were not quite following the instructions because they were not quite explicit. But the feeling was there."

As for emigre children, many have been exposed to contemporary Judaism. Some had religious training in the post-glasnost USSR, while others involved themselves in the numerous religious programs, activities and schools available as part of resettlement programs in the United States (Goldberg 1981; Gold 1994). In sum, the meaning and experience of Jewish identity for each generation of Russian Jews is often so different that it offers limited potential as a basis for family or community solidarity.

Migration Becomes Possible

The post-WWII exit of Jews from the USSR has been shaped by a complex configuration of political relations between the U.S., the USSR and Israel. During its entire history, the Soviet Union sequestered its population, strongly restricting immigration and emigration. Even short-term travel out of the country was carefully controlled and generally limited to a tiny elite of officials, athletes, scientists and performers.

Prior to the 1970s, very little emigration was allowed. During the entire decade of the 1960s, only 2,465 persons entered the U.S. from the USSR (Chiswick 1993: 262). However, in the early 1970s, the Soviets began to pursue a policy of détente and trade with the West. From the late 1960s to the present, American Jews have been very active in the Soviet Jewry movement which petitioned the Soviet government to allow its Jewish citizens to acquire religious freedom and settle in Israel. The movement was multi-dimensional and involved public protests when Soviet officials or performers came to the U.S., letter writing campaigns, efforts to make freedom for Soviet Jews a major consideration in U.S./USSR diplomacy and even organized visits to Jews in the Soviet Union.

From the late 1960s through the mid 1980s, various reports regarding the fate of "Refuseniks"—Soviet Jews who had applied to emigrate to Israel but were not permitted to do so—appeared with regularity in the Jewish and main-stream media. The Soviet Jewry movement benefited greatly from the cold war politics of the 1970s and 1980s because the image of millions of religion-seeking Jews being held against their will behind the "iron curtain" provided a powerful indictment of the Soviet Union.

Soviet Jews' supporters in the U.S. raised the issue of emigration and succeeded in linking a relaxed immigration policy to the "most favored nation" trade status granted the USSR in 1974. As a result, 51,000 Jews left the Soviet Union in 1979. Of these, 28,794 arrived in the United States. The decay in U.S./Soviet relations precipitated by the Soviet Union's invasion of Afghanistan resulted in a drastic reduction in the exit of Soviet Jews. During the mid-1980s, less than 1000 were permitted to leave yearly—and these tended to be very elderly. However, with the dawning of the glasnost period, immigration once again increased (HIAS 1995). Along with this rise in immigration came increased pressure from certain segments of the world Jewish community to resettle Soviet Jews in Israel rather than the U.S. (HIAS 1993).

Those who favored Israel as the sole destination for Soviet Jews cited Israel's need for settlers and the fact that they were personally invited to move there. The pro-Israel camp also argued that according to the Soviet "law of return" (a policy that permitted Soviet citizens to migrate to their nation of origin) Israel must be their destination since Jews' passports were stamped with the "Jewish" nationality. Soviet Jews who opted for other destinations were labeled *"Noshrim"* (dropouts) and were subject to inferior treatment by resettlement agencies in Europe. For example, it was the standard practice of Jewish immigrant aid agencies to provide emigres who chose Israel with rapid resettlement, while those who migrated to the U.S. had to wait weeks or months before placement (Panish 1981; Woo 1989).

Despite the pressures to settle in Israel, an increasing number of Jews chose the U.S., provoking fierce debates in the late 1980s. Pro-Israel forces demanded that the U.S. deny Soviet Jews group-level refugee status as a way to increase the movement to Israel. They had considerable success. In late 1989, the Bush administration revoked Soviet Jews' universal refugee status, and instead, only provided it on a case-by-case basis, favoring those with relatives in the U.S. (Ungar 1989; Woo 1989: B12; New York Times, Nov. 24 1989: 4; Tress 1991).

By the 1990s, Israel received far more Soviet Jewish arrivals than the United States, though the numbers entering both countries were enormous. In 1990, 182,000 Soviet Jews settled in Israel and 31,000 arrived in the United States (HIAS 1995). At present, Jews who wish to enter the States apply directly to the U.S. Embassy in Moscow. The number of Soviet refugees permitted to enter the U.S. (Jewish and otherwise) has been limited to 50,000 a year. Priority is given to selected groups of former Soviets that the U.S. Congress has identified as likely targets of persecution. These include Jews, Evangelical Christians, Ukrainian Catholics and followers of the Ukrainian Autocephalous Orthodox Church. Eligible persons with close, legal-resident relatives (parent, spouse, children, siblings, grandparents and grandchildren) in the U.S. are granted priority for entry. Members of these denominations who have immediate U.S. citizen relatives (parent, spouse or unmarried minor child) must apply as immigrants rather than refugees.

The new openness of the post-communist era has permitted Russian Jews to freely engage in a variety of religious and cultural activities for the first time in 70 years. Since 1988, almost 700,000 Jews have been able to leave, mainly for Israel and the United States. However, as Communist Party control of ideology has been replaced by freedom of expression, anti-Semites have also become increasingly active and virulent.

For example, in 1992, the Russian Nationalist Party published a manifesto featuring its 75 slogans. Of these, 52 were explicitly anti-Semitic or anti-Zionist (Gitelman 1992). A thirteen year old emigre now in Israel described his post-glasnost confrontation with prejudice in Kharkov: "I remember praying in the synagogue one night. I could hear this ugly chanting outside. Anti-Semitic slogans. Suddenly, the windows shattered—and the thugs were attacking us." (UJA-Federation 1995: 51). Most recently, Vladimir Zhirinovsky, the ultra-nationalist leader of Russia's Liberal Democratic Party, has become an important political force in the former Soviet Union. His many anti-Semitic remarks have given Jews and other ethnic minorities cause for concern. (Di Paz 1994:17).

The current climate in the former USSR—one characterized by impending economic crisis, social disorder, a revival of intolerant churches, and the rise of ultra-nationalism—appears to be a textbook example of a setting ripe for anti-Semitic outbreaks (Gitelman 1992). Accordingly, many Russian Jews still hope to leave for the United States, Israel, or other Western nations.

Choice of Destination

Why do so many Soviet Jews choose to settle in the United States rather than Israel? Emigres cite several reasons for their preference. These include greater economic opportunity, a higher level of national security, apprehensions about adjusting to the language and culture of Israel, and the presence of relatives (Brym 1993). They frequently refer to their children's future in selecting the U.S. because they see America as offering better educational and economic opportunities than the Jewish State (Simon 1985a; Orleck 1987). Parents claimed that while they had no personal objections to military service in Israel, they nevertheless wanted to protect the younger generation from involvement in war. (For a group who paid a great human price in WWII, this is a major consideration). Indeed, since the time of the Persian Gulf war of 1991—when Israel was attacked by Iraqi SCUD missiles—the arrival of Jews from the former Soviet Union has dropped precipitously in Israel, while remaining stable in the United States (HIAS 1995).

National and ideological factors also shape Soviet Jews' resettlement decisions. Soviet Jews are accustomed to identifying with a large nation and so prefer exchanging one superpower for another, as opposed to moving to a tiny country, which for many, has a total population surpassed by that of their former city of residence. Ideologically, many feel that Israel is too socialistic and religious, and consequently, that its government takes excessive control over citizens' private lives. "It's very, very socialist" said a Los Angeles emigre. "Israeli bureaucracy is world famous. Obviously, being a Soviet Jew, I had enough of bureaucracy." Others preferred the religious pluralism of America to Israel's state religion, where, as one man put it, "Their religion and their civil life are very close—almost like the communist ideology and the civil life in Russia."

While emigres had clear reasons for entering the U.S. instead of Israel, for many, the decision not to go to Israel continued to occupy their thoughts for years after settlement here. In fact, their first trip outside of the U.S. was often to the Jewish State. Reflecting some of the same ambivalence is the number of Soviet Jews now living in the U.S. who were initially settled in Israel. One colorful example is Marina Waks, a Beverly Hills based musician and composer who has performed in a variety of settings including the half-time show of the Superbowl. Despite her Russian origins, she is married to an Israeli immigrant and generally associates with Israelis rather than fellow Russians. Finally, it should be noted that a growing group of Jews from the former Soviet Union have settled in neither Israel nor the USA. Over 40,000 now live in Germany (Tress 1994).

DAILY LIFE FOR JEWS IN THE FORMER SOVIET UNION

Soviet Jews' views of life in the U.S. and their styles of adapting to their new home are rooted in their Soviet experience. Although they left the USSR as refugees and dislike a great many things about their former home, at the same time, most retain a degree of fondness for the culture, language, landscape, and accomplishments of the Soviet Union. A former concert pianist, now an x-ray technician, puts it this way: "You see, we are Jews but we related a lot to all of the Russian music, Russian culture, Russian theater, and literature. Not the church itself, but to the culture surrounding it."

Work and Family

Soviet Jews were proud of their ability to "make do" and enjoy a high standard of living in the USSR despite the anti-Semitism, war, shortages and purges that they had endured. Often, they became skillful manipulators of the system, and described their easy access to luxuries such as a car, a dascha (summer house), Western and Japanese consumer goods, and a rich cultural life featuring frequent visits to the opera, ballet, and symphony. An engineer recited how, through savvy, adaptability, and exchanging favors at work, he had developed the *blat* (influence) and *sviazy* (connections) to get the benefits and opportunities required to make life more comfortable and improve life chances for his children. "I could make favors to people and they, of course, returned. It was usual thing in Russia, it was the way for survivors. If not, your life is very hard. Especially Jewish people, they are flexible, and they can find ways to get some privileges. Its Jewish nature—because of Jewish history."

As Erving Goffman pointed out in *Asylums*, his classic study of total institutions, the sense of accomplishment a person derives from obtaining scarce privileges or goods through unconventional means is often more valuable than the actual possession of the good or privilege in itself (Goffman 1961). In maintaining a decent standard of living, a Soviet Jew is able to prove the strength of his or her character and an ability to triumph over adversity. This "culture of savvy" is retained by many Soviet Jews in the United States. It provides motivation in times of difficulty and contributes to positive feelings about secular Jewish identity. However, this outlook also has detrimental effects on emigres' communal life. Because Soviet Jews are so invested in individualistic and conniving solutions to problems, they often avoid formal, collective approaches to adaptation and community formation. A strong basis of Soviet Jews' ability to cope with their environment is found in the family. Due to the shortage of housing endemic in the former USSR, it is common for extended families of 3 or 4 generations to reside together in very close quarters (Orleck 1987). Further, because the birth rate among Soviet Jews is low, a small family size makes for a great deal of parent-child interaction (Simon 1983).

In contrast to American children who are socialized by peer groups, Soviet youth—Jewish and gentile alike—are more involved with kin (Hulewatt 1981). Relatives provide young Soviet Jews with political/bureaucratic influence as well as emotional support. I interviewed a young emigre who, despite her excellent record, was unable to secure admission to higher learning in her hometown of Kiev. She described how a relative living in Moscow utilized connections so that she could gain admission to a technical institute there. In general, families were a key source of social support for Jews in the former Soviet Union.

The Experience of Anti-Semitism

Every emigre I interviewed admitted the existence of Soviet anti-Semitism, but they disagreed about its nature and effects. The most common experience of prejudice was in the realm of career advancement. Soviet Jews who sought high status positions confronted institutional anti-Semitism. That is, even if they never experienced personal hostility, they knew that opportunities for themselves and their children were limited.

The role of institutional anti-Semitism is verified by data on Soviet Jews' enrollment in higher education. While the Jewish population of the USSR remained relatively stable between 1960 and 1970, the percentage of Jews in institutions of higher learning dropped from 3.2% in 1960 to 1.9% in 1970 (Simon 1985a:8). Younger emigres, like 34 year-old Zigmund, told me that they had to go to great lengths and mobilize all kinds of connections in order to be admitted to a university.

Many had been turned away despite achieving outstanding high school grades and gold medals on graduation exams. When they demanded an explanation, officials offered fabricated excuses. Mark, for example, was vigorous enough to commute the 30 kilometers to his high school by bicycle. Yet he was denied admission to a technical institute because of his alleged "poor health." Others, like Zoya and Paulina, reported having to abandon the hope of entering stimulating and prestigious occupations such as academic research or medical practice in favor of more mundane fields—like transport engineering or factory inventory control—that were still open to Jews.

Those who managed to gain access to professional training continued to confront obstacles to advancement, facing rejection when they sought jobs and promotions. A physician from Moscow put it this way: "Being Jewish is a great hindrance to advancement and promotion in a chosen field of work. That remains with you during all your working life." (Greenbaum 1985: 79-80). An electronic engineer described his confrontation with anti-Jewish quotas imposed by the Soviet bureaucracy: "I wanted to continue my education and get a promotion in my field. But as a Jew, I could not go above a certain level. It's not so much anti-Semitism among the people I worked with—I had good relations. But my bosses were limited with what they could do. It was Brezhnev time—it was State anti-Semitism. It wasn't much from the people. This is what is so outrageous—is that it's a State anti-Semitism, they just impose it."

Although educated and ambitious Jews living throughout the USSR confronted blocked mobility, the experience of more personal forms of discrimination varied by region. Emigres from Moscow, Leningrad (now St. Petersburg), and Odessa claimed they encountered little direct hostility. Indeed, Rabbi Boris claimed that Moscow Jews experienced "a little more freedom" because Soviet policy demanded tolerance in order to make "a good showing for visitors" to the capital city.

Both personal and institutional anti-Semitism was the fate of Ukrainian Jews, especially those from the Republic's capital, Kiev. Ukrainian Jews endured daily insult and harassment. An emigre from the Ukrainian port city of Odessa recalled rampant anti-Semitism during his business trips to Kiev. "When I came to Kiev, I took a bus from the railway station or the airport. And I asked myself 'How long will it take before I hear something about Jews?' And usually, it took only 15 or 20 minutes and I would hear something already."

EMIGRATION: MOTIVES AND MEANS

Motives for Emigration

While many Jews cite anti-Semitism as a motive for leaving the former Soviet Union, emigration was generally the result of a complex of "push" factors that encouraged exit as well as the "pull" extended by desirable Western locations. Prior to the fall of communism, push factors included personal and institutional anti-Semitism, blocked mobility, a low standard of living, and a repressive political environment. Since that time, economic collapse and fear of violence rank highly.

Pulls that motivate emigration include political and religious freedom, the presence of friends or relatives overseas, a high standard of living, the availability of resettlement services, and a stimulating social and cultural environment. Aware of ever-changing policies towards their group, Jews from the former Soviet Union also realize that the "window of opportunity" to migrate may slam shut at any time. In this sense, the possibility that migration may be restricted in the future is itself a motive for exit.

Soviet Jews almost universally claim that their children's future—not religious freedom—was their primary reason for emigrating. Many Soviet Jewish parents told me of their willingness to sacrifice their own relatively secure status and the easy retirement of their parents in order to improve their children's life chances. Andre, for example, spoke of a desire for his son to "grow up as a normal member of society."

Several emigres offered ideological reasons for leaving the USSR. Mark, a computer programmer from Kiev, described his evolution from patriot to dissenter. "I remember when I was in high school, if the Soviet government was challenged, I felt like I was being personally attacked. But as years passed, I learned that it was wrong to drive tanks into Czechoslovakia, Hungary, Afghanistan, and Poland. We knew that the people who fought back were right. How did I learn this? I think all intelligent people in the USSR knew it. We would seldom discuss these things directly, but we could pick it up through the odd joke or comment."

And, of course, anti-Semitism also played a role in awakening Soviet Jews' opposition to the Soviet Union. In the words of Zigmund: "The degree of anti-Semitism in Russia is, in general, high, but in Ukraine, in particular, it is very bad. It was completely destroying our lives. We could not live out our expectations. Eventually, it became very destructive to our mental health. I kept asking 'Why'? and eventually, I started talking about immigration."

Regardless of the unpleasant conditions they endured in the USSR, emigres described how permanently leaving their homes for an unknown future in the U.S. was a frightening prospect. Several told how they reached a mental state that allowed them to overcome such doubts—they simply "needed" to be outside of the USSR. In the words of one man: "When I left, I said, that's it. I don't care what's going on other places. I just don't want to be over there anymore."

In contrast to these impassioned and ideological reasons for leaving the former Soviet Union, other emigres offered less dramatic motives for exit. For example, a Los Angeles taxi driver described how his interest in jazz music caused him to develop a fascination with the West which culminated with his emigration. Similarly, when a sports journalist got into a job-related conflict with his supervisors, he opted to start a new life by joining his sister who had settled in Texas.

In the post-communist era, it is now possible to assess Jews' opinions about migration. A 1993 survey of Jews in Moscow, Kiev, and Minsk found that of those who planned to exit, 59 percent would leave for economic reasons (especially their children's future), 33 percent due to fear of political instability, anti-Semitism, or violence, and 8 percent to keep the family together (Brym 1993: 14).

Images of American Life

Despite their plans to migrate permanently, Soviet Jews know very little about the country to which they are moving. Because of restrictions on information, this was especially the case among the first wave of emigres who came before the downfall of the Soviet Union. Moreover, the few available sources of information about the U.S. were generally biased. "For many Soviet Jews, their only understanding of American life was derived from rock music, movies, and sensational literature. Marya recalls how a dog-eared copy of Jaqueline Susann's *Once is Not Enough* was passed from hand to hand in Leningrad. 'Inside ourselves,' she remembers, 'we knew it was a distorted picture of American life. But it offered up everything forbidden by Soviet censors—drugs, homosexuality, rich living. In a way we wanted to believe that was America—pure abandon'" (Orleck 1987: 291). Many elderly emigres were familiar with "Genry Fonda" (Russians pronounce "H" with a "G" sound) because his movies, notably "The Grapes of Wrath," reflected an ideological outlook and view of the United States that was acceptable to the Soviet government, who thus authorized their translation and distribution for the Soviet populace.

Short-wave radio broadcasts from the Voice of America and the BBC were another source of information. However, because they were part of the West's propaganda effort, they were highly biased. Finally, word of mouth reports from Jews already in the States—often second or third hand—were similarly rose-colored. They often portrayed the ease with which consumer goods such as cars, food and houses could be acquired. (One bit of gossip explained that in America, you could trade a frying pan for a used Chevrolet).

Images of America created within the Soviet Union—such as newspaper and magazine articles and textbooks—were steeped in Marxist rhetoric. While complementing America's technological achievements, they were also rife with discussions of capitalism's social problems. The following excerpt from a Soviet textbook (given to me by a San Francisco emigre) describes the American city where its owner settled: "Near the Golden Gate Park is the Haight-Ashbury

District, an abandoned middle-class neighborhood made famous by the influx of so-called "hippies" during the 1960s. Tourists have learned to avoid the . . . district . . . so dirty and dangerous that a wealthy San Franciscan says: 'I wouldn't drive through it even in the daytime with my car doors locked.' In the Golden Gate Park dozens of policemen on motor cycles try to discourage purse snatchers" (Tomakhin 1980: 157).

While Soviet citizens learned to be skeptical about the content of official publications, they couldn't help but believe some information. In fact, when they actually confronted the reality of American social problems—crime, violence, homelessness, and the like—emigres realized that there was a kernel of truth in what they had read.

The Process of Emigration

Prior to the fall of communism, when Soviet Jews applied for an exit visa—an act considered traitorous in the USSR—they became *persona non grata* and had to live on the margins of society for months or even years before they were permitted to leave. But simply applying to leave did not mean that an exit visa would be granted. Some applicants received clearance rapidly, others after lengthy delays, and still others not at all. Emigres claimed that the Soviet government intentionally treated visa applicants in this unpredictable manner in order to avoid accusations of discrimination while simultaneously obstructing attempts at second guessing by a politically astute populace.

Ironically, it not was until they applied for the exit visa that most Soviet Jews really became persons in need of refuge. During this period, potential emigres were frequently fired from their jobs, and consequently, were deprived of the resources needed to lead a normal life. They were then forced to survive in any way that they could, relying on savings, support from friends, or by picking up informal work. Doctors became night watchmen, engineers became handymen, and students who had been expelled from the university worked as tutors. An emigre with a Ph.D. in electronic engineering described how, prior to applying to leave, he re-

order to save the reputations of his co-workers, and supported his family as an on-call electrician until the exit visa had
been approved.

To obtain an exit visa, emigres had to get statements of
non-indebtedness and permission from their parents and
former or current spouse, regardless of the individual's age
or current relationship to the relative. Since having relatives
go abroad was harmful to a Soviet citizen's reputation, the interactions required to gain consent were often difficult. And
a relative's—such as divorced spouse's—refusal to grant permission could delay one's exit indefinitely. Further, "when
parents provided consent, they too were viewed as 'traitors'
and they too were harassed." This encouraged entire families
of Soviet Jews to exit together (Drachman and Halberstadt
1992: 67). Not surprisingly, a very high proportion of Soviet
Jewish families are multi-generational and, for a migrant
population, they are exceedingly elderly.

Despite the complex political machinations surrounding
their exit, Soviet Jews were often able to make extensive prep-
arations before applying to leave. Many sold their posses-
sions and hired an English tutor. The application for an exit
visa was, in itself, a politically complex process. An engineer
from Leningrad who had been employed in a low security
position within the Soviet defense industry carefully timed
his application to leave to coincide with a 1977 meeting on the
Helsinki Human Rights Agreement. He surmised that government officials would be so preoccupied with the meeting
that they would quickly approve his application in order to
clear their desks. From his office in San Francisco, he described the results: "It just worked. They let a whole lot of
people out without checking thoroughly. After we got out, I
met several others who also had a security clearance."

Prior to 1988, when permission to go abroad was finally
granted, emigres took a train to Vienna, where they stayed for
about a week while initial processing took place. From there,
a small percentage flew directly to Israel. A much larger
group traveled to the outskirts of Rome, where they remained for two or three months while their settlement to the
U.S. was arranged. Because the Soviet government limited
the amount of money and goods that emigres could take out

of the country (only about $100 in Rubles was permitted), the interval in Italy was endured on a minimal budget. Finally, when plans for resettlement to the U.S. were complete, Soviet Jews flew to a pre-selected destination where they either joined relatives or were sponsored by the local Jewish community.

After October 1988, Jews in the former Soviet Union applied for refugee status to the U.S. Embassy in Moscow. When they received permission to enter the U.S., they traveled directly there, thus avoiding lengthy stays in Europe. Because immigration is freer now, it often takes the following chain-like form. First, a nuclear family, including parents in their 30's or 40's and children, move to the U.S. (often to a community where earlier-arrived relatives have already settled). Then, a year or so later, when this family has established itself and found work, one or both sets of grandparents will enter with the purpose of providing child care for their grandchildren.

As a result of recent improvements in international communication and movement, emigres can now choose if and when they will exit. Consequently, major political developments—such as the Persian Gulf War, events within the former Soviet Union, and changes in the American economy—appear to have important effects on the number of Jews who leave the former USSR for the U.S., Israel, or other destinations.

CHARACTERISTICS OF RUSSIAN JEWISH REFUGEES

Soviet Jews are well-equipped for the task of adjusting to American life. They are skilled, educated, and possess urban experience. They also receive refugee status from the U.S. government and are therefore eligible for a variety of resettlement services, training programs, cash assistance, and permanent resident status in the United States. Finally, due to Soviet policy (prior to the downfall of the USSR) and family preference since that time, the unit of immigration for Soviet

Jewish refugees is frequently an intact family (Simon 1985a; Panish 1981; Jacobs and Frankel-Paul 1981).

Russian Jews are among the most aged of all immigrant or refugee groups to settle in the U.S. Their average age is 35.5 years, with 17.5% age 65 and over (HIAS 1994: 14). [For purposes of comparison, the average immigrant to the U.S. was 29 in 1990]. Family size for this population is very small. A recent study found that the average Soviet Jewish household consists of 3 persons (Simon 1983: 503). Nearly all emigre families have two or fewer children. Women outnumber men and are significantly older, indicating their greater life expectancy as well as the effects of WWII.

Russian Jews are highly educated, having attended school or college for an average of 13.5 years, greater by one year than the average educational level of the U.S. population (Simon and Brooks 1983, Statistical Abstract of the U.S. 1984). In addition, a very high proportion of Soviet Jewish women are accustomed to working outside the home, often in lucrative professional and technical occupations. The result of this pattern and the generally high educational levels for all emigres is that family income is substantial for a recently arrived immigrant group (Gold 1994: Table 13). A 1989 survey of Soviet Jews who had been in the U.S. at least eight years found their average family income to be $34,000 (Kosmin 1990; ORR 1984).

HIAS (the Hebrew Immigrant Aid Society), the agency that resettles Russian Jewish refugees, is long established, well-funded, and works in conjunction with other Jewish and public agencies such as Jewish Family Services, Jewish Vocational Services, and Jewish Community Centers to offer a variety of services. These range from initial settlement to job training and placement, social activities, religious socialization, and mental health programs. Due to the efforts of these various agencies, Russian Jewish immigrants are generally resettled in middle class neighborhoods rather than the inner city enclaves that are the usual location of recently arrived immigrants.

The resettlement of the most recent wave of Russian Jews is partly facilitated by the communities of their earlier arriving countrymen (and women) who entered the U.S. in the late

1970s and early 1980s. While some friction occurs between the two groups, the newly-arrived take good advantage of the already established services, community activities, and Russian-language infrastructure (stores, restaurants, doctors, religious programs, media) in Soviet Jewish neighborhoods. Because Russian Jews are resettled by American Jewish agencies, they are distributed among cities that already have sizable Jewish populations. These include New York, Los Angeles, Chicago, Boston, and San Francisco. While the greater New York City area has the largest population of Soviet Jews in the U.S., with more than 100,000 emigres, the two locations of my fieldwork—Los Angeles and San Francisco—are sizable emigre colonies as well. The Southern California community of between 18,000 to 25,000 is approximately the same size as that in Chicago and hence is among the top three nationally, while the Bay Area population is about 15,000.

CONCLUSIONS

Jews have a long and ambivalent history in Russia. While they were subjected to personal and institutional anti-Semitism from the period of the tzars, through the communist era and until the present, at the same time, many are strongly attached to the nation, culture, language, landscape and way of life of the region, and have done quite well there. Their Russian experiences of oppression and accomplishment deeply color their understanding of life in the United States and their patterns of adaptation to this new setting.

2

FAMILY PATTERNS

INTRODUCTION

The family is the most important social unit among Jews from the former Soviet Union. Over the centuries, the Russian Jewish family has adapted to provide its members with support, comfort, and motivation in a hostile environment. It continues to fill these functions among emigres in the United States.

The Wisemans: A Case Study

Several key issues in the lives of Soviet Jewish emigres become evident when we consider the experience of a fairly typical family, the Wisemans. I met members of this family about six months after they came to the U.S. in spring 1982. I visited them weekly for about a year and a half, and then sporadically until late 1990. The Wisemans, mother, father and two sons, settled in San Francisco because Mrs. Wiseman's brother and his family were there. The parents, Victor and Bella, had lived most of their lives in Kiev, the largest city in the Ukraine. Both speak Yiddish (it was Bella's first language) as well as Ukrainian and Russian. Born soon after the revolution and in their late 50s when they entered the U.S., they were among the last cohorts of Soviet Jews able to receive a religious up-bringing. Victor had a Bar Mitzvah and Bella had attended a Yiddish-language Jewish school in her village before her family moved to Kiev when she was 9 years old. As youths, both Bella and Victor believed in communism and the Soviet system. Among the belongings they brought from Kiev are pre-WWII pictures of themselves with other idealistic young Jews who, in their words, were "building communism". Also among their belongings were Victor's military decorations earned in "The Second War." As was the case for most Soviet citizens, the war meant great hardship for the Wisemans. Because the Ukraine was captured by the Nazis, Bella and her parents spent several years in Uzbekistan, an eastern region of the Soviet Union that the Nazis were unable to conquer. Mr. Wiseman was a soldier and fought in the famous Battle of Stalingrad. His family was not evacuated during the war and died at the hands of the Nazis.

The Wisemans have two sons. As of 1982, Mark was 29 and Louis was 22. Although both were excellent students, neither was granted admission to university or an institute in Kiev. Both, however, were able to attend the Institute of Railway Technology in Moscow, partially through efforts of Mrs. Wiseman's brother who lives there. Mark's education included the use of American mainframe computers that had been acquired during the detente period between the U.S. and the USSR in the 1970s. Because of the applicability of his skills to the American economy, he was able to find several good jobs after a relatively short period in the United States. He was referred to his initial position in the data processessing center of a grocery chain by the San Francisco Jewish Vocational Service. Shortly afterward, he found a better job in the computer department of a small city, but continued to work for the grocery firm during the evening. Russian engineers older than Mark often had much more difficulty in finding work because of their lack of experience with modern computers. [In a bizarre application of Marxist doctrine, until the mid-1950s, Soviet ideologues banned certain subfields of computer science because they reflected "bourgeois values." This, along with economic factors, meant that computers and even advanced calculators were relatively rare in the Soviet Union until the late 1980s].

Louis shares his older brother's interest in electronics. His first year in the United States was spent as a student at the Computer Training Institute, his tuition paid by refugee benefits. He found the computer school easy, graduated early, and found two part-time jobs as a computer technician. Having established California residency, Louis attended San Francisco State University where his courses in electronic engineering were much more challenging. After graduation, he found a job about 50 miles from his parents' home in Silicon Valley. Here, he rents an apartment and visits his parents on weekends.

During their first several years in the States, both sons complained about the difficulty of getting along with their dependent parents. Mark, the older son, was dutiful and maintained a cordial relationship with mother and father. Younger Louis, however, often expressed anger towards his parents and brother, blaming them for the disruptions of his life created by leaving the USSR. An aggressive young man and the best English speaker in the family, Louis sometimes acted officious, ridiculing his parents and brother. In other moods, he bought them gifts and tried to help Papa find a job. Prior to his moving out, Louis's behavior ranged between that of an extraverted know-it-all and a brooding child. However, after establishing his independence, his interactions with the family grew more civil, if less frequent.

Victor and Bella Wiseman take a great deal of interest in their children. While they hope for the boys' success, at the same time, each additional step towards independence the sons make is a source of further worry. Like many older emigres, both parents complain about their health and make frequent visits to the doctor. In Kiev, Victor was a sewing machine repairman while Bella worked as a factory accountant. Because of problems with health and English, neither of the parents work in the States. Instead, they keep busy by attending English classes, visiting relatives and neighbors, and participating in religious activities. Bella received post-secondary education, her husband did not. She is in better health than Victor and has more relatives here than he does; her brother and his entire family—children and grandchildren—

live only doors away, while Victor has no blood relatives, save his sons, in the U.S.

In general, Bella is quicker than her husband in understanding the details of American life. She has learned more English and is the "instrumental" head of the family, dealing with social agencies and the like. She also spends a great deal of time in the kitchen experimenting with American foods. Without a job and with fewer social contacts than she had in Kiev, Bella now finds that cooking is one of the only activities she can engage in which provides some sense of continuity with the past. On one occasion when I was discussing cars with Mark and Louis (the Russian word for car is *machina*) Bella patted her Soviet meat grinder and claimed "this is my *machina*".

Initially, both Wiseman sons felt a lack of companionship and isolation when they came to this country. Their many relatives provided support, but they had few real friends with whom to share their successes. Most Soviet Jews claim it takes years to develop truly close friends and sorely miss their past relationships. Before he married Mina, Mark often socialized with other young emigres, but felt that many of his companions were below him in education and moral development. Perhaps to forget their loneliness, the sons spend long hours working and studying. Both have held 2 jobs simultaneously and frequently work 10 to 12 hours a day.

As time passed, Mark met and married Mina, a woman from Odessa about ten years his junior. Unlike the Soviet practice of women working outside of the home, Mina stayed home with their son. Following the tight family patterns common to Soviet Jews, in marrying, Mark became enmeshed in Mina's family circle, and moved with her into the same Oakland apartment building—nicknamed the Moscow Hilton—where Mina's parents and several other emigre families lived. Since Mina's parents were much younger than Mark's—in their late 40s—they were both employed and contributed both money and effort to Mark and Mina's well being.

KEY FEATURES

Three social conditions have been especially important in shaping the experience of Soviet Jewish families like the Wisemans in the United States: the patterns of family life prevalent among middle class urbanites in the Soviet Union (a group to which the overwhelming majority of Jews belonged prior to their exit); their unique demographic makeup; and their Jewish ethnicity. The overlapping effects of these several factors makes Russian Jewish families inordinately close and intimate in comparison to those found among middle class Americans, Jewish and Gentile alike.

This closeness, coupled to the high levels of education, skill, and resourcefulness that characterize the Russian Jewish population endows the family with impressive resources for helping members adjust to the new setting. Yet, precisely because of the intense attachments that characterizes emigre families, trauma and conflict can be extreme when established patterns and roles are disrupted or become ineffective after migration.

Family Patterns in the Former Soviet Union

While observers often attribute Soviet Jews' adaptive behavior to their Jewish ethnicity or the immigrant experience, many family patterns they exhibit in the U.S.—notably closeness, intimacy, and extensive parental involvement in children's education and career choices—were typical of urban Soviets, regardless of their ethnic origins (Shlapentokh 1984).

In the period after the Russian revolution and during the Stalin era, the social engineers of Soviet society sought either to reduce the influence of the Russian family (which they held to be hopelessly conservative and oppressive of women), or co-opt it into service of the state. However, since the early 1950s, the Soviet family has developed into an independent social unit that preserves a sphere of life beyond the reach of government, supports the expression of genuine views, and, through warmth, spontaneity, and sincerity, allows its members to "acquire what they are deprived of in official life" (Shlapentokh 1984: 73).

The social and ideological influence of the Soviet family is demonstrated in various surveys conducted in the 1970s which revealed that it was the most important initiator of opinion-formation for Soviet citizens, outweighing other sources such as schools, the mass media, professional associations or labor unions. In addition to its importance as the locus of nurturence and ideology, the Soviet family was also a fundamental source of economic well being. Because it maintained an environment rooted in intimacy and trust, the Soviet family "played the central role in relations surrounding the second economy—which was an enormous, unofficial system of distributing goods and services. . . . Members of families trust each other completely about their activities in this realm (illegal production, bribery, etc.) and serve as important connections in helping each other get what they need" (Shlapentokh 1984: 73-74).

The Soviet family was crucial in determining children's career outcomes. Family members provided resources through legitimate channels (such as drilling students and hiring tutors) and also exerted influence with authorities to help secure additional opportunities. It is paradoxical that in a society which officially repudiated the idea of class distinctions, parents were often obsessed with securing security and upward mobility for their children to a far greater degree than is common in capitalist nations. According to a Soviet sociologist: "The overpowering desire to see children moving up the ladder of prestige pushes Soviet parents to make sacrifices to ensure their offspring the best education and best jobs . . . In fact one of the most widespread forms of corruption in the Soviet Union is that connected with the settling of children's affairs" (Shlapentokh 1984: 89-90). Children were understandably tied to their parents who were so essential in helping them acquire the material necessities of life as well as their future occupations and careers.

Demographic Effects

Patterns of family composition that have their roots in the Soviet Union also reinforce intimacy and mutual involvement among emigres in the U.S. Because of Soviet housing shortages and the desire to maximize available resources for children's mobility, family size was small—with most families rarely having more than one or at the most two offspring. Soviet grandparents retired early (women at 55, men at 60) and were often extensively involved in the lives of their children and grandchildren with whom they lived (Markowitz 1993).

Urban families in the former USSR tend to maintain an extended (as opposed to nuclear) configuration and exhibit deep involvement across generations. Prior to 1989, Soviet emigration policy worked to insure the emigration of intact multigenerational families by encouraging or even mandating the exit of elderly emigres along with their more youthful offspring (Drachman and Halberstadt 1993). Nearly one in five (17.5 percent) who entered the U.S. in 1993 were 65 and older (Gold 1994). Even though the various States of the former USSR have significantly reduced their control over emigration, the high proportion of elderly among Jewish migrants has continued. Families bring over their aged members in order to remain intact, care for children, and provide an environment more secure than that of the former USSR.

The relative closeness of family members from different generations is noteworthy, especially for a highly educated group. In American families, generations are often 30 years apart. In recent decades, American women—particularly those of the educated middle class—have been marrying and giving birth to their first child later and later in life, often in their late twenties or early thirties (Baca-Zinn and Eitzen 1987: 232-233). By the time a middle class couple is getting established, their parents are often close to retirement age.

In contrast, Jews in the Soviet Union often get married and have children at a much younger age, often in their early twenties. (As the Wiseman family shows, this pattern is not universal). Pragmatic in outlook, Russians seldom devote years to the development of "a true self" (Hulewat 1981). Moreover, Russians generally have very different ideas about courtship than Americans and feel that it is appropriate, especially for women, to settle down and get married early in life. [Emigres point out that there is no direct translation for the generally wholesome American expressions "boyfriend" or "girlfriend." The closest Russian equivalent is akin to "mistress" in meaning and, consequently, sounds somewhat prurient]. The housing shortage endemic in the former Soviet Union precludes both the freedom offered by establishing a separate household as well as the need to defer life plans while saving up to pay for a residence.

As a result, both in the former USSR and in the U.S. as well, parents and children tend to be much closer in age than American families of similar education. It is not uncommon to find four generations residing together. The labor force participation of parents and children overlaps for many more years than is the case among the American middle class, allowing employed parents to be actively involved in shaping their children's careers (by offering advice, exercising influence or working together in family businesses) and facilitating multiple earner households. Generational closeness has a pronounced effect on mothers and daughters, who often share many interests and develop very deep relationships.

In the United States, many emigre families cling tenaciously to their Soviet-based ideas about marriage. A Moscow-born entrepreneur told me: "My daughter is 17—she goes to Fairfax High. She has her boyfriend and wants to get married and start her own family. I understand her, so we are supporting that. We are not so worried about college now." This continued emphasis on early marriage for women maintains Soviet-based patterns of family closeness, but in the American context can thwart a young woman's ability to obtain a higher education and consequently, adversely affect her career options.

A final contrast between emigres families and those of the American middle class has to do with their drastically different values concerning individuality. American families highly value autonomous functioning, with parents and children carrying out separate lives (Bellah et al. 1985). However, both the Russian family and Soviet society encouraged a more collective, mutually dependent pattern (Hulewat 1981; Cunningham and Dorf 1979). Anthropologist Fran Markowitz (1993) asserts that Soviet Jewish families almost lack boundaries between parents and children. Mila, an emigre college student, expresses this as she compares the "Russian" attitude about family loyalty and privacy with that of an American acquaintance, Melissa, who shares her family secrets with outsiders: "I'll give you an example. Melissa, she always tells me about how her sister's on drugs and all of these family problems and this divorce and that divorce and on and on. Whereas Russians don't go around saying these things. It might be like rumored around, but you don't go telling your friends 'Oh my god, my brother got arrested'. You know what I mean?"

The Jewish Dimension

The particular experience of emigres as Jews further supports close ties among family members. Scholars examining the social patterns of Eastern European Jews have long noted closeness as a dominant characteristic. Among this group, parental dedication to and gratification from their children's achievement (called *nachis* in Yiddish) is a central feature. In fact, comparative studies of ethnic families in the U.S. have revealed that Jews tend to visit their parents more often than other ethnic groups (Farber et al. 1988).

Soviet Jew's need to insulate their children from anti-Semitism made the family an institution of paramount importance. This was evident in career-related realms of education and job search. "Believing (or wishing to believe) that their on-the-job contributions canceled out at least part of the negative effects of being Jewish, they guided their children to follow in their footsteps and pursue a high status career. From early on in their children's development they urged them to study hard, obey the teacher and conform to the rules of the group. They themselves brought small gifts to teachers and school directors, thereby smoothing the path of their children's advancement. As the children matured, parents planned their future by capitalizing on personal . . . connections to insure a place for them at an institute of higher learning" (Markowitz 1994b: 9).

Parental dedication to children's success, a pattern associated with former Soviets in general and Jews in particular, is indicated by their almost universal claim that the children's future was their main reason for leaving the Soviet Union. Such was the case for recently widowed Zoya, who asserted that the U.S. offered an opportunity for a single parent like herself to support her children in a manner inconceivable in the former USSR. "In Russia, my husband was very sick for more than two years. All the last year of his life, I supported the family. It was real hard, almost impossible. But in this country, one working person can support their family."

Once in the United States, American Jewish organizations responsible for the resettlement of Soviet emigres reinforce family links as they place recent arrivals with established relatives. In fact, because the California settings where I conducted my research are highly desirable locations for emigre resettlement, the only way an emigre family will be located there is if they have relatives in the community. In such cases, distant relatives often assist one another in providing sponsorship, spending several thousands of dollars on people they barely know in the process. (Of course, emigres initially resettled in other regions can and often do move to California despite their lack of relatives in the Golden State).

Hence, a variety of factors, including patterns of late Soviet family life, the demographic make up of emigre families, Soviet migration policies that facilitate the export of multiple generations, and the traditions of Eastern European Jewish life all contribute to the close knit and enmeshed nature of Jewish families from the former Soviet Union. In comparing their families to those of native-born Americans, Jews from the former Soviet Union generally emphasize their greater closeness, intimacy, and family centeredness. Developed partly as a survival technique in the Soviet Union, this family pattern often facilitates the rapid adjustment of emigre family members.

FAMILY SUPPORT IN THE U.S.

Once in the U.S., emigre families generally maintain their patterns of child-focused mutual involvement and support.

Paulina, a computer programmer, described how she tutored her daughter. "Here, I'm sure if I don't help my kids, they will be in bad shape. A few weeks ago, in science, my daughter had to understand electricity. She had question about generators and motors. She didn't know about them. I spent maybe one week explaining them to her. And then, her test was excellent." A college senior discussed the Russian parental obsession with children's accomplishments. "All Russian families totally push their kids. You have to play instruments, you have to play sports, you have to be the best in school, you have to be a doctor, a lawyer, an engineer. You know what I mean, like the top. Where Americans are sort of like lax—You know, 'You do whatever you want'".

As many scholars have noted, patterns of family solidarity can be valuable resources in immigrant entrepreneurship (Light 1972; Kim 1981). During fieldwork, I interviewed the owners of restaurants, beauty parlors, retail shops, and a variety of service enterprises, all of which relied on family-based resources in order to adapt to their new setting. A taxi driver living in Los Angeles described how his entire family was immersed in an entrepreneurial lifestyle: "I'm proud to own my own cab and I am satisfied. My wife has a little business too. A beauty shop in Beverly Hills. Sometimes she even does hairdo for TV stars. We have plans to get bigger operations in the future."

Despite the risks associated with entrepreneurship, small businesses are valued by emigres as a source of economic security for their families. Soviet Jews who are accustomed to lifetime employment expressed a great deal of concern over the frequency with which American workers lose their jobs. By passing on a business, they hope to ensure financial independence for their children. For example, Sophia's wedding present from her father was a guaranteed income in the form of three taxis along with the medallions (licenses) required for their operation.

Commenting on their high levels of familial interconnection, emigres sometimes point out that there is no word for privacy in Russian. Even in college, they maintain closer ties to their parents' household than do American youth. Svetlanna commuted 40 miles daily through rush hour traffic (in a new Nissan, purchased by her father) in order to live at home, while Mila stayed in her dorm only on weeknights, taking leave of the campus every weekend. Marina, a college senior who came to the U.S. at the age of 4, contrasted her Russian ideas about family with those of her American roommate, Jennifer. "When people ask me, 'Where is your home?' I would say my parents' house. All Russians are like that. But if you asked Jennifer where she lives, she would say her dorm, her apartment. She goes home like a visitor."

PROBLEMS FACED BY RUSSIAN JEWISH FAMILIES

All is not smooth going in Russian Jewish families in the United States, however. Because families tend to be extended and multi-generational, different patterns of adaptation may occur within the same unit, disrupting established patterns of interaction. Many older emigres who had positions of importance in the former Soviet Union have lost their social rank. Women must adopt new family roles. Teenagers who quickly master American customs and the English language are charged with managing the entire family's interaction with the outside world. Parents and grandparents who had hoped to guide their children towards maturity find that their Soviet experiences are of little use in the U.S. Adolescents who are pulled from a familiar social environment at a vulnerable time in their lives sometimes encounter more adjustment trauma than their parents. And, a shortage of suitable co-ethnic marriage partners challenges emigres who would like to establish their own families.

Reversal of Breadwinner Roles

Because wives and/or children sometimes find employment more easily than fathers, many Russian Jewish families experience a reversal of traditional "provider" and "recipient" roles. True, Russian Jewish women are used to being employed outside of the home. However, the American context continues to test their abilities. Part of the problem can be traced to the fact that emigre husbands (like Russian men generally) are famous for their virtual non-involvement in domestic chores, regardless of their wives' occupational commitments. Svetlanna pointed out "My father is like that. He won't do anything. He knows how to make a mess, but he won't clean it up." Eveta, a resettlement worker who is herself a Jewish immigrant from Poland, respected Soviet women's ability to deal with the multiple challenges of life in the United States: "You see, I admire Russian women much more than Russian men. On one hand they seem oppressed and exploited by the men. On the other hand, they do heroic things. They work, they cook the dinners, they clean up, they do it here and they did it there. They keep the family stability and the burden of immigration in on their shoulders. Women from Eastern Europe are tremendous."

Reversals of provider/recipient roles also affect refugee children who become breadwinners and/or translators and must assume adult responsibilities at an early age. This is especially so among recently educated Soviet youth—engineers, computer operators and the like—who have skills that are highly compatible with the American economy. Young emigres frequently expressed displeasure about their obligations. Many resented being deprived of the extended adolescence and consumption patterns which constitute major elements of the "California lifestyle." Some reacted to their burden in passive-aggressive ways—by spending little time at home, avoiding parents, refusing to eat mother's cooking, or adopting liberal social and political values to which parents object. Others attempt to hasten their education so that they can become more independent.

Status Loss

Ironically, the high levels of education and previous occupational prestige that characterize Russian Jews cause certain parents to become especially dependent upon their spouses or children (Simon 1985a; Hulewat 1981). Some who had a prestigious occupation in the Soviet Union are reluctant to accept a less desirable job in the U.S., and so remain unemployed. An emigre I met while teaching a job-finding class described his determination to regain the job title of Chief Engineer. Meanwhile, he refused to accept less-than-desired work. This put tremendous pressure on his wife who had to support the family, and on his teen-age son who felt he had to get good grades so he could eventually establish connections and prestige for the family in American society.

One way Russian Jewish families deal with problems of role reversals and status loss is through a "status leveling" process. Those who feel that they are at a disadvantage in social ranking frequently bring up information that discredits apparently successful family members in order to make the relationship more equal. Consider the reaction of the Wiseman family to its most successful member, cousin Igor. Igor, age 30, has a well-paid job as a mechanical engineer, has gone on several business trips, and owns a new car as well as many other consumer goods. Igor also speaks almost perfect English, masking his slight Russian accent with a Western "twang." While occasionally commenting on Igor's accomplishments, Bella and her children more frequently work to neutralize his achievements with mentions of his crazy driving, how much weight he has gained, his garish taste in music, clothes and entertainment and his enormous phone bill, inflated by calls to his girlfriend still in Kiev. At least within the family, this process of "status leveling" resolves some problems of status loss and role reversal.

Dependent Elderly

Soviet Jewish families express concern over the adaptation problems of elderly members, who frequently gave up stable lives in order to accompany their families to the U.S. Many came specifically to care for their grandchildren. However, by the time the grandparents arrive—perhaps two years after the settlement of their offspring—the Americanized youngsters have developed a great deal of independence and lost much of their ability to speak Russian. Usually, they are unwilling to be supervised by their aged kin. When Zoya, a civil engineer, initially came to the U.S. as a single mother, her children were often left to fend for themselves as she established her career. When her parents joined her two years later, she was living miles from the West Hollywood enclave where elderly Russians congregate. Isolated in the suburbs, Zoya's parents felt un-needed by their grandchildren and had few possibilities for creating a social network of their own. She described their situation: "My parents used to do real important jobs. They both were engineers. Now neither the kids nor I really pay enough attention to them. I work a lot, and my kids don't want to be supervised. For our first two years here, the kids were on their own. Now my parents want them to ask before they get something from the refrigerator or a drink of water."

In addition to the challenges of work and raising her own children in new society, Zoya is also confronted with the terrible unhappiness of her father, who complains that old age and isolation in California is as miserable an experience as that he endured in Stalin's camps during the 1930s. She described hearing his disparaging comments about life in the States as "a knife in the heart."

Fortunately, the experience of elderly emigres is not universally dismal. Many who settle in Soviet Jewish enclaves develop an active life. Even those with few co-ethnic ties sometimes adapt well. Paulina described how her parents, who initially came to help care for her children, have learned to enjoy English classes with elderly Korean and Chinese immigrants in a local community center. "My mom and dad help with my kids, but it's boring for them because they are not very old and they want to live. So, when we moved to Hacienda Heights, they began to attend adult school. It's very close; they don't have to drive. And this school, it's like another life for them. They have very good teachers, good friends. Now, my mom's English is good for a person her age and she loves Chinese food."

In the United States, the advice of elderly parents is no longer as valuable or relevant as it once was. Parents and children alike recognize that the parents' experience of growing up in the Soviet Union provides few insights into the concerns of children who are living in California. A woman who had been a concert pianist in Odessa describes this experience: "I cannot tell my grand daughter 'when I was 15' because she says 'when you were 15, you were in Russia.' Not only a generation gap, it's a gap of different culture."

Generational conflicts like these are especially intense among highly skilled groups like Russian Jews. Sasha, a 35 year-old emigre, was making $30,000 a year as a computer programmer two years after his arrival in the U.S. His position contrasted dramatically with that of his parents who lived with him and knew almost no English, did not drive, and were unemployed. Consequently, Sasha had to provide them with economic support, transportation and translate for them at the same time as he managed his own career and family life. To offer his parents some independence, the family lived in a Russian-speaking neighborhood far from his job, thus requiring Sasha to make an 80 mile commute. He comments on the demands created by his dependent parents: "With my parents, it's not that they are just from a different country, they are from a different world. There are so many things they just don't understand. I have to take care of them. But I have my own life too."

Emotional Demands on Children

Emigre parents who have experienced status loss often attempt to succeed through their children. The result: they put a great deal of pressure on their children to achieve a prestigious and successful lifestyle to demonstrate that the decision to migrate was a wise one. "Parents could and did view their offspring as extensions of themselves," writes Fran Markowitz, who studied Soviet Jews in New York. "Parents often attributed to their children the same desires, wishes and motivations as they had and interpreted their children's accomplishments as their own" (Markowitz 1994b: 9).

A resettlement worker I knew commented that Soviet parents often realize that their children are under much more pressure than the native-born. "They say 'our kids always cried and were always nervous and tense.' And they said this was because 'We were so tense and so crazy about them that we made them crazy.'" She went on to observe that due to pressures and problems in adjustment, many Russian Jewish adolescents have little in the way of a life of their own: "I have seen such cases of depressing loneliness in a 20 year old boy or girl. I know this one beautiful 22 year-old. She spends most of her time at work and then she spends time with her family. There is no outlet to go out because she doesn't know how to."

Emigre children spoke ambivalently about their close relations with parents. On the positive side, parents are supportive and generous, but, less happily, they are also demanding and controlling, especially with daughters. Parents often assume that they will continue to exercise influence over their daughters well into adulthood, play a major role in selecting their husbands, and always live nearby. Svetlanna attributed the premature marriage of her sister to this sort of parental coercion: "That's why my sister got married. My mom just pressured her to the point where she couldn't take it. She was going to run away. And actually, now that my sister didn't marry a Jewish person, the pressure is on me." Similarly, a UCLA student complained "My parents don't understand that I am an American now. Nobody lives with their parents after marriage. I want to have my own life." (Fruchtbaum and Skager 1989: 14).

Svetlanna described how her parents fostered a dependency relationship. "My mom will get up and she'll start limping and say 'I'm so tired, can you wash the dishes?' If I say no, she'd look at me like 'You're going to let your sick, poor mother go and wash the dishes?'" In contrast, an older student recalled her desire for autonomy as a passing phase: "When you're 15, 16, 17, you sort of rebel, you go along with your friends and, you don't do what your parents say. But then you get into your 20's and you get closer to your parents and you sorta like do everything they say."

Because they want to adapt to American life rapidly (often in response to parental pressure), some emigre youth follow a strategy that may ultimately foster downward mobility. In the Soviet Union, higher education was the most direct way a Jew could avoid extended military service and achieve a decent standard of living. In the U.S., young emigres have a variety of career opportunities—often in self employment or the business world—which at least in the short term, require less effort and offer greater economic rewards than the pursuit of advanced degrees. Ambitious young emigres who confront family pressure sometimes reject lengthy periods in universities and head directly for the labor market.

Dependent Youth

If some emigre youth feel pressure to get ahead because their parents have not succeeded in this country, others confront problems because their parents have achieved economic security with relative ease. Based upon their own experiences, such parents often think that learning American customs is not an essential for upward mobility and may be intolerant of their children's adoption of American practices and values. In their desire to protect children from alien influences, they may end up fostering excessive dependence and prevent children from learning the social skills needed to maintain normal relationships with Americans (Aronowitz 1984; Hulewat 1981). Some even encouraged their children to leave school and join them in the family business.

Adjustment to American Schools

Relying on their solid pre-migration preparation, emigre students make remarkable strides in American schools. In a 1991 comparison of the 12 largest immigrant groups in New York City public schools (based upon students who had been enrolled for 3 or fewer years in grades three though 12) students from the former USSR ranked first in reading scores, second in math, and fifth in English. What is more, their reading and math scores were much higher that those of all students in New York City schools, including the native born (Gold 1994: 29). Yet, despite (and perhaps because of) their strong preparation, emigre children do confront academic problems in the United States. After all, young emigres were torn from familiar surroundings and forced to struggle to build a new life in urban California schools, where even the native born find it increasingly difficult to maintain physical safety, let alone graduate with a college-worthy record.

Schools in the former USSR are generally more rigorous than American schools and students attend a ten year (most recently eleven) rather than twelve year program. Soviet students begin studying advanced subjects such as calculus and biology before Americans and as a result, are academically years ahead of Americans of the same age. Because of the lack of structural congruency between the two educational systems, Russian students are frequently required to repeat earlier work. Needless to say, many emigre students find this to be discouraging. In the words of one student: "after one year I understand Russia is better in school. Before, I was interested in studying, but here, I realize that the (American) program is like in Russian grade 5 or 6." Students' frustration is compounded by the fact that their limited English ability prevents them from expressing themselves or demonstrating their advanced knowledge. In the words of one Los Angeles high school student: "English is difficult but work is easy" (Gold and Tuan 1993: 17). In this way, emigre students "become frustrated, and it is not surprising that some display aggressive acting out, absenteeism, vandalism and other behaviors bordering on conduct disorders" (Kozluin and Venger 1993: 69).

Many teachers, resettlement workers, and other authority figures in the U.S. are troubled by the behavior of Russian Jewish students who are accustomed to dealing with authority figures and bureaucrats in the Russian style. In the former Soviet Union, lower level officials who dealt with citizens were trapped between demanding clientele and powerful, upper-level bureaucrats. To ease some of this pressure, the system tolerated a high degree of flexibility and personalism in the delivery of services. Soviet citizens were not immediately impressed by authority figures and expected their service providers to be susceptible to influence and negotiation.

Because Soviets understand authority relations in this manner, American teachers and resettlement staff who work with Russian Jews may find themselves treated as equals rather than superiors. For example, Russian Jewish students openly disagree with teachers or counselors, claim that their suggestions or assignments are "stupid", talk during class or "ditch" (skip class) when the feeling suits them. Advice may be ignored or compared to information from other sources. An English as a Second Language teacher described her Soviet students as acting arrogant and belligerent in class: "Some of my Russian kids are really obnoxious. They think the work I give them is 'baby work' . . . that it's too easy. They act like I'm insulting them by expecting them to do the work, but they don't understand that I have reasons for giving them each lesson . . . they can still learn from the exercise."

Many emigre students see such "baby work" as a waste of time and unworthy of serious attention. "I think the main problem is just that we have a higher level of knowledge. You don't want to go to the next period if you know what they're going to do there. And if it's just boring, people don't want to come." (Gold and Tuan 1993:12)

Emigre youth often see rules as being subject to evasion. In the collectivist Soviet Union, individualism was not a key value, so copying or cheating on school work were not considered to be serious infractions. Hence, Russian Jewish students often appear aggressive, disrespectful or manipulative to American authority figures. However, when viewed in context, their behavior does not indicate some deep-seated arrogance, but rather reflects their indifference to American-style displays of respect.

Emigres, then, often experience their years in American high school as full of conflict and unwarranted delays which prevent them from achieving pre-set life goals. In response, some follow an alternative educational path. Having discovered that junior colleges will accept students without a high school diploma, they drop out to pursue what they see as the fast track to a college education. Some follow the correct procedures for withdrawal, others simply stop coming to school. However, if their plans to obtain the Associate of Arts (junior college degree) are thwarted, students find themselves lacking even basic English skills and a high school diploma and, are faced with few desirable options for employment.

To American teachers, these actions of Soviet emigre students often appear irrational. However, it is important to recognize that given their own understanding of the American educational system, the Soviets are taking what seems to be an active, appropriate, and practical path to achieve the personal and familial goals that, to them, are most pressing.

A Limited Choice of Marriage Partners

Given the relatively small number of young emigres and the diversity of this population, Soviet emigres experience considerable difficulty in finding appropriate marriage partners. This is especially hard for women because some families expect their daughters to be married by their early 20s at the latest. As Svetlanna said, "if you're not married by 22, nobody wants you. Why is it always the girl? The guy could be like 40 and not married and he's okay, you know, but the girl has to be married."

Vladim Gutmeyer, a physics student at an elite university, described his awkward blind date with a Soviet Jewish girl from a different class, regional, and cultural orientation than his own. "I guess she knew about me because my father is active at the Jewish Community Center. One day, she called up. It was kind of strange, but I agreed to come over. When I arrived, they had set out all kinds of foods and the girl and her family really tried to impress me. They were from the eastern part of Russia. It was sad, she was really looking for a husband, but we had absolutely nothing to say to each other. I was so glad to get out of their house."

Despite the scarcity of co-ethnic partners, few refugees are interested in marrying Americans. A social worker who resettles Soviet Jews comments: "They don't envision marrying an American because the customs are too different. And it's very surprising to me because some 18 or 19 year-old people say 'What would we have in common?' They already don't see the possibility of getting out of their ethnic group perspective."

As the free exit of people from the former Soviet Union has expanded, several informants claimed that marriage brokerage businesses have developed that pair young women in Russia with established emigres in the States in marriages of convenience.

CONCLUSIONS

Jewish families from the former Soviet Union are marked by a high degree of closeness and mutual involvement. These features, developed to survive in the Soviet environment, generally help members to adjust to American life. At the same time, close family ties and expectations often lead to conflicts as family members seek more personal autonomy and freedom than they were accustomed to before they migrated. Still, emigres remain committed to their time-tested patterns of family association, which manifest themselves in Los Angeles poolside condominiums in much the same way as they did in "Khrushchevskies" (1950s-vintage efficiency apartments) in Moscow.

3

EARNING A LIVING IN A NEW SOCIETY

INTRODUCTION

Jews from the former Soviet Union possess skills and resources which help them achieve economic self sufficiency in America. The most adaptable emigres are those who are immediately employable as professionals in the U.S. economy. Others command the technical skills needed to find jobs as mechanics, machine operators, musicians, dental technicians, carpenters, computer operators and the like. Even emigres whose home country occupation is not useful in the American context—classical accordion and balalaika players, coaches of sports not played in the U.S., journalists who have yet to master English, Leninist teachers of Russian history, computer-illiterate engineers—tend to be flexible once they become familiar with the demands of the American setting. Many make remarkable progress in learning English and applying themselves to the new environment.

For Soviet Jewish emigres, cultural and contextual obstacles are the greatest impediments to adjusting to the United States economy. Once they learn English and understand how the American job market works, they tend to do quite well. Government reports single out former Soviets for their rapid rates of withdrawal from refugee cash assistance (RCA). To quote from the *Office of Refugee Resettlement Report to Congress, 1993*: "The RCA utilization rate for the Soviets is the lowest of any large [refugee] group" (ORR 1993:24). The pre-migration economic environment is key to understanding the employment experience of Russian Jews. In the former Soviet Union, there was officially no unemployment, and job placement (as well as the whole Soviet economy) was centralized and government controlled. After completing his or her education, a worker was assigned a job, which could potentially last a lifetime. The entire process of finding employment in the U.S.—from the identification of job openings to creating a resume, applying for jobs, and going through interviews—is totally unfamiliar. On top of this, the job search takes place in a language, culture, and geographical setting that are equally exotic. Hence, Jews from the former Soviet union face great challenges in finding work in the U.S.

A large cultural gap also exists for those who become self-employed in the U.S. Until quite recently, private enterprise was prohibited in their country of origin. Nevertheless, a surprisingly large percentage of Soviet emigres have, like earlier generations of Jewish immigrants, set up their own businesses here.

BENCHMARKS OF ECONOMIC ADAPTATION

Education

Soviet Jews are highly educated and experienced in technical and professional fields. Data from several sources indicate that Jews from the former USSR have a higher average education than the U.S. population as a whole. For example, the 1990 Census found that 58 percent of former Soviets in New York City and 72 percent in Los Angeles County had one or more years of college.

Earnings

Barry Kosmin's survey of established emigres records that Soviet Jews in the U.S. experience rapid economic adjustment, resulting in an average family income of $34,000 in 1989 for those in the U.S. 8 years or more. The 1990 Census revealed that, with exception of those in the U.S. three or fewer years, Soviet Jews' incomes exceeded those of other immigrants and approached those of native-born whites.

While the average income of former Soviets suggests a generally successful merger into the American middle class, there is of course a wide range in the entire Soviet emigre population, from poverty to significant wealth. About 30 percent of those who had been in the U.S. for a year or less in June 1991 were receiving Refugee Cash Assistance (RCA)—a program for indigent refugees that provides benefits similar to those offered by welfare. With the exception of those in the U.S. three years or less in 1990, unemployment rates were low, under 7 percent in New York and Los Angeles.

The rates of labor force participation, employment and dependency on government support associated with a refugee population are important to policy makers because U.S. refugee programs were created specifically to make "employment training and job placement available in order to achieve economic self-sufficiency among refugees as quickly as possible" (Section 311, quoted in Murray 1981). Consequently, the good economic performance of Soviet Jewish refugees serves to demonstrate that further admissions will not be a drain on the U.S. treasury.

Women in Professional and Technical Fields

One economic asset of the Soviet Jews is the unusually high number of women with professional and technical skills. Indeed, there are more workers with former employment as "Professionals" or "Engineers" among the women than among the men. Sixty seven percent of Soviet Jewish women in the U.S. were engineers, technicians, or other kinds of professionals prior to migration. In contrast, only 17 percent of

American women work in these occupations (Gold 1994: 20-24). According to the 1990 Census, 29 percent of Soviet emigre women in New York City and 26 percent in Los Angeles County work as professionals in the U.S. Despite their high levels of education and professional experience, Soviet Jewish women earn 40 percent less than their menfolk and studies show they are less satisfied with their jobs (U.S. Bureau of the Census 1990; Simon et al. 1986).

Areas of Employment

Soviet Jews are finding jobs and earning a good living, but many are unable to meet their previous level of occupational prestige. A study of New York's Soviet Jewish community found that only about half of those who had held professional, technical and managerial occupations in the USSR, managed to find similar jobs in this country. Lack of job-related licenses and certifications, limited English language skills, and the incompatibility between certain Soviet and American occupations make it hard for many highly skilled emigres to get the kinds of jobs they would like and are trained for. For example, Eveta, who was a concert musician, now works as a respiratory therapist, Herman, trained as a civil engineer, owns an auto repair shop, Luddy, who was an economist, bakes bagels, and several former doctors support their families by driving taxicabs.

FINDING A JOB

Job-Placement Agencies

Nearly all Soviet Jewish immigrants start their job search with the assistance of a job referral office, often in a Jewish community agency known as the Jewish Vocational Service (JVS). This organization was created by the Jewish community during the 19th century to help their compatriots find work. Given the large number and unique needs of Soviet Jews in California, the JVS in both San Francisco and Los Angeles has developed programs and hired staff members specifically to aid Jews from the former Soviet Union.

Job placement activities are an especially important element in resettlement, because unemployed refugees are supported by government funds. One of the major legal responsibilities of the refugee resettlement system, as mandated by Congress in the Refugee Act of 1980, is to help refugees become economically self-sufficient. Job placement agencies like the JVS want to make the job finding process quick and efficient and encourage refugees to accept the first available opening. Emigres have other ideas. They want to find a prestigious and well-paid job. When job seekers are professionals, as so many emigres are, with university educations and years of experience, they strongly identify with their previous occupation, treating it as "the be all and end all of the . . . individual search for a social place and well being." In the former Soviet Union "Jews overcompensated for their stigmatized 'national identity' by pouring their energies into academic and professional pursuits. Some, members of the intelligentsia in particular, found in their work a means of escape from the unpleasantness of other aspects of the Soviet system" (Markowitz 1994b: 8). Understandably, they do not want to accept any job that comes along. Thus, agency staff and clients disagree on the acceptability of jobs as well as the amount of effort that should be expended in securing a position. Emigres consider placement workers lazy and unhelpful, while staff view their clients as overly demanding and inflexible.

A further complication is that recently arrived refugees without competence in English lack a full understanding of how the American economy and the employment process works. And many Soviet Jewish refugees have entered the U.S. job market in the early 1980s and early 1990s—in periods of recession and high unemployment—when jobs were relatively scarce. All of these factors—the need for jobs, the scarcity of job opportunities, and refugees' lack of understanding of American job-finding practices—come to a head during face-to-face interactions in the Jewish Vocational Service.

Some emigres interpreted their interactions with the Jewish Vocational Service in light of past encounters with the Soviet state employment agency, where desired services were delivered by bureaucrats in exchange for favors. Emigres who were not referred to jobs they liked sometimes assumed that agency staff were holding out in order to receive a payoff (Di Francisco and Gitelman 1984). Occasionally, emigres attempted to bribe staff or offer indirect payment in the form of contributions to the Jewish Federation.

Rather than following the suggestions of staff, some emigres try to acquire jobs through Soviet-style political machinations involving influence and connections. Emigre engineers attending a job-finding class at a Jewish Community Center repeatedly asserted that the best way to find jobs is through influence with the right persons. "Do you know the director of the Jewish Federation? We will talk to him. He could go to the president of a big engineering company, Jewish president, and tell him to hire some of us. There are only a few of us. He could hire one of us each week."

Zoya, who eventually found work as a structural engineer, explained how problems with job placement alienated her from American co-ethnics: "They [the Jewish Vocational Service] did not help me even a little bit. I found my first job myself. [They had] no real compassion for people. My boss, he is a Catholic. He helped me a thousand times more than any other Jew." Reflecting on Zoya's feeling of frustration, Boris, an emigre activist, commented "at that particular moment, counseling people represent the entire American Jewish community. As a consequence of misunderstandings and poorly handled job placements, emigres become bitter. Many are still not quite dying to affiliate themselves with the organized Jewish community."

Step–by–Step: The Job Search in Retrospect

With the exception of the elderly, nearly all of the adult Soviet emigres I interviewed were either working or obtaining an education in preparation for a career. Work, and finding good jobs, were on everybody's minds. Whether they were driving a cab, selling sandwiches, or performing surgery, Soviet Jews spoke extensively about their experience of getting a job.

In the USSR, where Jews confronted anti-Semitism, they knew that finding an appropriate career and position demanded effort and imagination. "There were a lot of ways to get what you required" a San Francisco entrepreneur asserted. "It was usual thing in Russia, it was the way for survivors. Especially Jewish people, they are flexible and they can find a place to get something they need."

Emigres described how they set about following a deliberate plan to learn English and develop the skills needed to find work in the U.S. They often used the phrase "step by step" to explain their efforts. For doctors—who are well represented among the emigre population—this meant that they pass tests in both medical knowledge and English competence. Engineers, another common emigre occupation, had a somewhat easier time since they only had to demonstrate their skills to employers rather than pass formal exams. Many Russian Jews had prior experience with computers. For them, becoming acquainted with American hardware, software, and technical terminology were necessary in order to find a job.

Paulina, now employed in the computer center of a university, described her experience of finding a job as part of a long-term process that began during high school in Latvia. "I originally wanted to be a doctor and I had very good grades. But Jewish people could not become doctors, so I went into computers. In Russia, I did programming for machine tools." After arriving in California, Paulina was happy to find her specialty in demand: "Programming is good. You can find a job easy. Only you have to know what you are doing."

For a fee, an established emigre offered to re-train Paulina for the American job market. However, Paulina and her husband (who had already found a computer-related job) decided to save their money and, in her words, "self-start" instead. So with the aid of books and a junior college (where she took "classes, classes, classes—word processing, data base, cobol, basic"), Paulina spent her first two years in the States polishing her computer skills while shuttling her children between public school and a synagogue day care program. Finally, when Paulina's parents arrived from Latvia to help with the kids, she told herself "okay, now I can try to find a job."

Because she was unfamiliar with the way to go about getting a job here, the job-search itself was more difficult for Paulina than acquiring job skills. She contrasted the simple process of finding a job in the USSR with the vastly more complex one of the United States. "In Russia, I was a good student. When I graduated, I went to the placement office and they said 'You go this day to there.' And I was very glad to get this job."

"But in America," Paulina explained, "first you have an interview! What does it mean, interview? What do you have to wear to the interview? What about your behavior? When we came, my sister and her husband explained how to open the newspaper, and they told us where you find the job advertisements, how to make a resume, and how to type a letter [of application]." Paulina confided that it was even difficult to get to the Jewish agency (The Jewish Family Service) where she attended several lectures on finding a job because it was such a long drive: "It was a challenge to go there. It was too far for me."

Assistance from the Jewish Family Service turned out to be extremely valuable. The staff taught Paulina about applying and interviewing for a job and how she should present herself—using concrete examples to reveal her positive attitude and demonstrate her abilities as a hard worker and "a team player." The agency ultimately helped Paulina obtain an interview and gave her the confidence to apply for a job that involved an unfamiliar brand of computer. Finally, two years after her arrival from the USSR, she secured a job that met her requirements.

In contrast to Paulina, other emigres realized that their previous occupation was not in demand in the U.S. and initiated new careers. Eveta, who had been a concert pianist in Moscow, became a respiratory therapist in San Francisco. Or take the case of Oleg, who recognized that he could not resume his vocation as an electrical engineer. Proclaiming that "the money doesn't smell," he accepted a less prestigious job as a mechanical draftsman that permitted his family to move to a better apartment. Svetlanna, a college student, told how her father who had been an engineer in Belarus decided on a new occupation in Los Angeles. "He didn't have the language skills—and by the time he'd go to school to learn them, who is going to support us? So he started working in auto mechanics. Now he owns several cabs."

SELF-EMPLOYMENT

Self-employment is a means by which immigrant Jews have traditionally supported themselves and their families, from the German Jews of the 1850s and the Eastern Europeans of the 1880-1920 era to contemporary Israelis and Iranians (Goldscheider and Zuckerman 1984; Howe 1976; Glazer and Moynihan 1963).

Data from the 1990 Census indicate that a sizable proportion of Soviets are self-employed: 15 percent in New York and one fourth in Los Angeles. The Los Angeles figure puts Soviet Jews among those ethnic groups with the highest rates of self-employment. Although many of these are professionals like doctors, dentists and engineers who practice independently and hence count as both professionals *and* self employed, this does not in itself explain the Soviet Jews' high rates of involvement in small business.

Motives for Opening a Business

As illustrated by Horatio Alger stories, American popular culture glorifies self-employment as an ideal economic situation. In reality, small business ownership is a risky and difficult way to earn a living, requiring long hours of dull work, responsibilities that do not end at 5 o'clock, risk of robbery, and a high chance of failure. As recently arrived refugees, Soviet Jews suffer additional disadvantages. They lack many of the resources needed for running a successful business—investment capital, secure credit histories, U.S. business experience, and knowledge of the English language and American culture.

Given these many disadvantages, why do Soviet Jewish refugees become entrepreneurs? The growing body of research on ethnic economic activity points to several reasons. As Ivan Light's (1980; 1984) typology suggests, they do so partly because the have certain cultural attributes, but more importantly, because they suffer disadvantages in the labor market (Light 1980: 33). At the same time, they have certain resources that help give them a start and contribute to their business success.

Culture Theory

Cultural theory claims that certain ethnic groups, such as Jews, Chinese, Japanese, Greeks, Armenians and Parsis (Bonacich 1973: 583) possess cultural traits that encourage and facilitate their participation in business activities. These groups are said to have access to cultural institutions for raising capital, controlling family labor, and ensuring economic cooperation (Ward 1986; Min 1988). Many hold religious or cultural values similar to the Protestant Ethic that emphasize characteristics like future orientation, acquisitiveness, and thrift which are conducive to entrepreneurial activities. Also, it is suggested that certain ethnic groups see small business ownership as a prestigious and worthwhile activity.

What Light calls orthodox cultural theories go so far as to claim that certain groups such as Jews and Chinese are, by nature, business-oriented. Reactive cultural theories argue that the skills and orientations which encourage and facilitate small business ownership "emerge from the minority situation" (Light 1980: 34). In other words, reactive theories are context-based, stressing that cultural traits become important in encouraging business activity when other factors in the social environment make business enterprises an appealing and viable prospect. As we have seen, Russian Jews have many experiences and cultural attributes that could contribute to their involvement in self-employment. These include flexibility, a goal-directed, future-time orientation; experience in currying personal ties and manipulating bureaucracies, an ability to get along with various social groups, a desire to function independently, literacy, mathematical competence, a family structure that can provide resources and assistance, and a tradition of self-employment. Because Russian Jews' tradition of self-employment is closely related to their history of oppression and exclusion from other kinds of work, their cultural orientation towards entrepreneurship is marked by both orthodox and reactive dimensions.

Cultural theory applies most directly to the experience of emigres who opened small businesses out of choice, despite opportunities for employment in the larger economy. Such was the case of several Soviet Jews who had found high paying employment as structural engineers but preferred to work in small business instead. One went into auro repair, another bought a restaurant, and a third purchased a retail electronics store. In another case, an emigre coach chose to become an insurance salesman. "I worked just maybe a month as a coach for a girls' school. You know, I just quit because I didn't see my future in that. I decided "What are Jewish people doing when they don't have a profession? They should sell something."

Culture theory does a good job of explaining the actions of immigrant entrepreneurs who are excited about and skilled and resourceful in business. It does less well in helping us understand the experience of refugees who open businesses solely as a source of income. Their experience is better explained by disadvantage theory.

Disadvantage Theory

Disadvantage theory asserts that certain immigrant and minority group members go into small business because they are disadvantaged in the general labor market due to poor English, inferior education, lack of American credentials and licenses, and discrimination (Kim 1981; Min 1988). Disadvantage does play a major role in motivating Soviet Jewish refugees to enter business. In fact, many of the business owners I contacted indicated that disadvantage was a reason for opening their operation (Gold 1989). These respondents included engineers who owned bagel shops, auto repair businesses and real estate concerns, accountants who owned bakeries, and educators who sold dry goods.

I found little evidence to indicate that self employment was a direct alternative to unemployment (Light 1972; Min 1984). Few Soviet Jewish refugees can move from being unemployed to owning a successful business. Running a business requires capital, knowledge, and commitment. Soviet Jewish refugees who opened businesses only out of desperation often lacked these resources. Hence, businesses that were established by refugees who were short on skill and assets, solely for the purpose of creating a job, were likely to fail. Grisha Goldberg, a structural engineer from Moscow, is a case in point. Having searched for work as an engineer for three years, both in Chicago and in the San Francisco Bay Area, Grisha was convinced by his friend Arkady Levy to join three other Soviet emigres and one American in starting a business. They leased a windowless, dingy basement adjacent to a university, remodeled it, and opened a "beer and sandwich" restaurant. Almost immediately after start up, Goldberg and his partners realized the business was destined for failure and put it up for sale. On many days, receipts were less than $100. The final blow occurred when they were caught selling beer to minors. Because they refused to pay a $700 fine, their liquor license was revoked by the state. At last, a buyer was located. After agreeing to reduce the price by $25,000, it was sold. Despite each partner's losses in the thousands of dollars, they were grateful to be out of business. Disillusioned by this attempt to become an entrepreneur, Goldberg renewed his search for employment in engineering.

Instead of being an alternative to unemployment, small business among Soviet Jewish refugees was more often an alternative to underemployment. Refugees experienced their disadvantages in terms of the low quality of employment which was available. While initial jobs were considered undesirable, nevertheless, they provided refugees with cultural socialization, English language proficiency and investment capital.

Ethnic Business Resources

Despite the many obstacles faced by Soviet Jews when contemplating self-employment, emigre entrepreneurs also possess various advantages by virtue of their status as refugees and their connections to the Soviet Jewish community.

Funds

One advantage Soviet Jewish refugees have is access to funds. This may sound surprising since they entered the U.S. with few financial assets and thus did not come with the capital required for business start up. Lacking stable jobs, credit histories and collateral, they were unable to obtain small business loans from banks. Community connections have been frequently used to provide alternative sources of capital. Typically, these are informal social circles of family and close friends. These networks range in size from the two persons (mother and uncle) who helped finance Alex Kogan's electronics shop to the more extensive network that Tony used to establish a restaurant in a San Francisco office complex. "I have over 30 relatives in San Francisco" Tony said, "and they didn't have a choice [about giving money], they were my relatives . . . I just said 'I gotta have it.' Probably, I'd do the same thing if somebody wanted my support."

On the whole, the networks refugee entrepreneurs rely on for capital are small and involve relatives or close friends. Social solidarity in the Soviet Jewish community exists within localized subgroups and not among the entire refugee population. Because Soviet Jews often avoid involvement in formal organizations, capital formation networks are generally informal.

Some social scientists suggest that formal, institutionalized, and community-wide social solidarity is required for effective funding of immigrant businesses. The present case shows that this is not so. Despite their small size, the networks refugees rely on are often effective. A major reason is that the people in them have relatively high earnings because so many Soviet Jews have found work in high-paying occupations. I interviewed several professional Soviet Jewish couples—engineers, doctors and the like—who earned over $100,000 a year. Having relatively few expenses, these families had significant disposable income available to aid relatives. Because refugees' capital formation networks were small and intimate, they offered a degree of flexibility and responsiveness that was helpful to starting entrepreneurs.

Not that informal business networks do not have disadvantages. Since emigres' networks are rooted in personal trust and cooperation, when relations sour, businesses suffer. Several refugees opted to sell out when they could not get along with partners. Svetlanna described how her father was swindled by another Russian Jew that he had too easily trusted: "My father owned a body shop with another Russian guy. His partner sold half of the business but didn't tell my father. The person that bought it started moving in and saying 'Oh, we thought this whole place was sold, not just half of it.' My father went 'what's going on? You can't come into my business. . .' They (other emigres) are very malicious people. They'll cut your throat for five dollars (laughter)."

Emigre entrepreneurs sometimes felt that co-ethnics lacked the resources that American business associates could provide. A successful restaurant owner stated: "I'd rather not get involved in something serious with Russians to say truthfully. Only because I believe they don't have enough experience yet and in many cases, connections. Let's face it, that we need sometimes." As emigre entrepreneurs became better established, they were able to obtain credit from banks and investors. Indeed, most large scale operations were supported by these more traditional sources of capital.

Labor

Another factor important to Soviet Jewish entrepreneurs is in their access to labor. There are three major sources: family members, co-ethnics, and workers from other immigrant populations. All of these workers are part of ethnic labor markets, but only people in the first two categories have special ties to emigre employers.

Soviet Jewish entrepreneurs in California definitely used family labor, but this practice was far less common than among other recent immigrant populations such as Koreans, where family labor is almost a universal feature of ethnic entrepreneurship (Light and Bonacich 1988; Min 1988). Many times, family members are unavailable to help out in businesses because they already have good jobs. Affluent Russian Jewish entrepreneurs often limit their children's involvement with the business, hoping that higher education will lead to a more prestigious professional occupation (Gold 1989). When the business grows, employees are selected from the larger labor market rather than the immediate family. Two emigre college students, Mila and Svetlanna, both came from families who owned businesses (a medical office in one case, a body shop and taxi franchise in the other). Each said that she had occasionally "helped out" with the family business, but that her involvement was minimal. Both sets of parents made it clear that their daughters' first priority should be their education.

Soviet Jewish refugees also hired non-related, co-ethnic employees. The ability to tap workers in the ethnic community has long been noted as an asset to immigrant business owners (Glazer and Moynihan 1963; Bailey and Waldinger 1992). Far from seeing jobs in businesses owned by co-ethnics as rewarding, Soviet Jews looking for jobs almost universally preferred to work in large American companies that, they felt, offered better wages, fewer hours, more security, health benefits, and opportunities to learn English.

It would be a mistake, however, to assume that refugee employers are harsh exploiters of co-ethnic workers (Howe 1976; Lyman 1974). My field work and interviews indicate that direct exploitation of co-ethnic workers was generally moderated by ethnic customs. Relations between many owners and workers are best characterized as "paternalistic exploitation" (Portes and Manning 1986). True, emigres—especially those with few other job options—worked for lower wages or longer hours than non-ethnic workers would accept. At the same time, Soviet Jewish employees enjoyed benefits from co-ethnic employers that they would not receive from American businesses. Many Soviet Jewish employees got "under the table" wages from refugee employers that would not jeopardize their Refugee Cash Assistance, AFDC, or unemployment benefits (Arax 1987). Refugee proprietors I interviewed (like the business people of many immigrant nationalities) were also less concerned than most American employers with enforcing strict discipline among workers. Bosses did not mind if co-ethnic workers kept irregular hours or worked on their own projects while on the job.

For instance, Genady, who owned an auto repair shop, permitted his mechanics to restore their own used cars during slow periods.

Refugee workers are often in a stronger position than other immigrant workers because they are entitled, as refugees, to various benefits when they arrive in the United States including, instruction in the English language, job training and most significantly, Refugee Cash Assistance (RCA) (Rose 1986). (Prior to 1981, the period of eligibility for RCA was a full 3 years. Recently, this period has been cut to about 8 months.) In their very first years in the country, when other immigrants, desperate for jobs and without knowledge of the English language and American society, are most exploitable by ethnic employers, refugees are supported by public assistance and do not need to work. This contrast between refugees and immigrants is especially dramatic in California, where benefits are generous and numerous undocumented entrants aggressively seek employment. Finally, because of their high levels of education and skill, relatively few Soviet emigres were interested in accepting the kinds of positions generated by co-ethnic businesses—generally low paid labor or service jobs—for more than a short period.

At the same time, several emigre business owners, including some of the most successful, avoided employing co-ethnic workers because they lacked the skills and characteristics needed in their enterprises. In one case, an employer had 15 unionized, native workers in his laundry plant. He felt that the high quality work provided by his well-paid staff gave him a competitive advantage. In another case, a couple employed a Chicana seamstress in their clothing outlet. Not only did she help out with the sewing, but she also solved communication problems with Spanish-speaking customers.

More typically, Soviet Jewish employers claimed that emigre workers would challenge their authority in ways Americans would not. An engineer who ran his own electronics firm stated that when he hires American employees they are easy to manage, but when he employs co-ethnics, they are jealous and challenge his authority: "With Russian employees, they think, 'Why is he president and I am just a worker?'

and psychologically, I understand that. But it is very distracting."

Soviet Jewish entrepreneurs with labor needs—like many other immigrant business people in California—increasingly rely on Mexican, Chicano and Central American workers (Gold 1992). Entrepreneurs associated several advantages with Latinos. They were physically strong and worked very hard, often lacking legal residency, they were easy to control, and as cultural outsiders who did not speak Russian, they were unlikely to open a competing enterprise or use their job as an opportunity to engage in "inside job" crimes such as embezzlement or protection rackets. Finally, Latino workers could not demand favors based upon common ethnicity. In contrast to their positive characterizations of Latino labor, Soviet Jewish employers describe co-ethnic workers as disrespectful, overly ambitious, and generally more difficult to manage than Latinos.

The ethnic bonds which unite owners and workers, then, are a mixed blessing for Soviet Jewish entrepreneurs. Owners can find co-ethnics to work in their enterprises, but ethnic bonds oblige bosses to extend special privileges to ethnic workers, especially to relatives. The ability of recently arrived refugees (those most disadvantaged in the job market) to collect refugee cash assistance makes them less ripe for exploitation by co-ethnic employers than is the case among recently arrived immigrants who are ineligible for such benefits and hence must find immediate employment.

Co-ethnic Consumer Markets

Co-ethnics are an important sources of customers for the goods and services of some emigre businesses in refugee neighborhoods. These include food stores and medical offices, as well as nightclubs, barber/beauty parlors, furniture shops and clothing stores that cater to a Soviet Jewish clientele.

Soviet Jewish enterprises in California have changed over time. Until the late 1980s, most were directed at the general population rather than other Soviet Jews, mainly because there were not yet enough refugee customers. Soviet Jews were resettled throughout the U.S., impeding the development of large-sized ethnic enclaves like those that support Vietnamese, Cuban and Korean ethnic businesses (Gold 1992; Portes and Bach 1985). Since the glasnost era, large numbers of Soviet emigres have continued to settle in areas like West Hollywood and Brooklyn's Brighton Beach. Thousands of Soviet Armenians and Pentacostalists have added to this consumer market (ORR 1989). In these neighborhoods, a growing number of Cyrillic-language signs offer Russian-style products to the local community. As relations have warmed between the U.S. and the former Eastern Bloc, more Russian and Eastern European products—food, beverages, cultural goods and the like—are now available. By 1994, West Los Angeles featured a number of groceries—ranging from tiny delis to full-sized supermarkets—that offer a whole variety of goods imported from the former USSR and Eastern Europe.

Among the emigre population, there is an obsession with food, rooted in Eastern European Jewish culture and nurtured by decades of shortages in the former Soviet Union. Entrepreneurs find a huge demand for quality cuisine, the more gourmet and specialized the better. Generally, money is no object. As first wave refugees (who arrived in the late 1970s) have become established, they have largely abandoned shopping at American and even Russian-style supermarkets, and instead patronize a series of small, European-style specialty shops, delis and greengrocers where they purchase high quality produce, pastries, imported salmon, sturgeon, caviar, sausages, sweets, and fine champagnes for cornucopian meals. Similarly, several restaurants offer lavish fare, drinks, and live entertainment where flashily dressed Russians spend long evenings in celebration.

Soviet Jewish real estate agents, accountants, investment counselors, tax preparers, doctors, lawyers and dentists also utilize ethnic consumer markets. Doctors have been especially dependent upon ethnic customers because they have found it almost impossible to obtain the certification in a medical specialty which is required for employment in most hospitals and HMOs. Private practice, then, became the only option for employment. Taking advantage of refugees' eligibility for Medicare and Medi-Cal (government health programs), the practices of refugee doctors have been directed towards refugee communities.

Physicians and other professionals have provided a windfall for other sectors of the ethnic economy, such as medical supply companies, office buildings, dental labs, pharmacies, and, most notably, ethnic media industries whose newspapers, magazines, cable TV programs, and ethnic "yellow pages" carry their advertisements. In 1991, 50 of the 108 advertisements in the *1991 Los Angeles Russian Language Telephone Directory* offered various medical services.

A Soviet-trained physician described the role of the ethnic media in her practice: "I got my office and I placed my advertisement in our (Russian) newspaper. I was working in a famous hospital in Russia, so a lot of patients from Russia, they know this institution very well. I even have some of my own patients from Russia."

Some successful Soviet Jewish entrepreneurs have directed their operations towards the larger society or other ethnic groups. For them, assimilation has been an important business skill. They need to know, for example, about the larger society to make decisions about store location and marketing. In catering to non ethnic consumers, they have found access to more customers, less competition, and have been able to charge higher prices than would be possible with a refugee clientele.

Whatever the market, Soviet Jewish businesses have faced competition from entrepreneurs from other ethnic groups. Southern California's largest purveyor of Russian-style foods—Ron's Market—as well as several bakeries are owned by Armenians. Israelis, Iranians, and various Asian-American groups sell food and other consumer goods that appeal to emigre consumers' tastes.

Even though the businesses of ethnic outsiders drain customers from refugee-run operations, they also attract customers to ethnic shopping districts and make available goods and services that benefit Soviet Jewish enterprises. For example, cars purchased from non-emigre dealers are often fueled, repaired, washed, and insured through the services of Russian entrepreneurs. In general, co-ethnic customers offer a consumer market of increasing importance for Soviet Jewish business people.

Connections to the Greater Jewish Community

Jewish entrepreneurs from the former Soviet Union enjoy several advantages through their connections to the established American Jewish community. Despite occasional strains, relations between established American Jews and recently arrived Russians are generally positive, with individuals in both groups feeling a bond on the basis of their common origins (Markowitz 1993). Because emigres are often resettled in Jewish communities, they find themselves among native-born Jewish neighbors who are at least somewhat familiar with and sympathetic to them.

Following a long tradition of self-help, Jewish-American entrepreneurs often hire recent emigres to work in their businesses. Soviet Jews already know many of the cultural, religious, dietary and linguistic patterns of American Jews and thus make suitable employees. In addition, American Jewish customers are interested in sampling the goods and services offered by their Russian-born cousins. In a process known as ethnic succession, established American Jews planning to retire from small business ownership often sell their shops to recently arrived Russians. In many typically Jewish occupations such as jewelry, delicatessens and retail sales, former Soviets have taken over the occupations held by earlier generations of American Jews.

Many American Jews are concerned about retaining a Jewish presence in traditional Jewish neighborhoods where ethnic institutions are located and many elderly and low-income Jews reside. For this reason, they often welcome, and Jewish organizations have encouraged, the settlement of recent Jewish immigrants from the former USSR as well as Israel and Iran. The transfer of businesses in such locations is often expedited by the common ethnic origins of both buyer and seller. In some cases, the acquisition of business, homes or other goods by Russian Jews is even financed by funds from Hebrew Free Loan—a Jewish social service agency (Tenenbaum 1993).

In summary, Soviet Jewish refugee business owners have definite economic, organizational and motivational resources by virtue of their status as refugees and members of an ethnic community. These resources are vital to refugee entrepreneurs because they often find themselves competing with business owners who have more capital and better connections in the U.S. than they do.

CONCLUSIONS

The experience of Soviet Jewish refugees in entering the U.S. economy is generally a positive one. Emigres tend to be skilled, educated, and resourceful. Many are able to maintain their previous occupation in the U.S. Others develop new vocations, either by finding jobs in existing companies or by setting up their own businesses. Emigres' economic adaptation is greatly facilitated by community connections. American Jews provide English training and a variety of job placement services. While some emigres complain about these services, job placement agencies play an important role in getting jobs for Soviets. Communal funds sometimes help emigres with business start-up and other costs. Emigres' entry into traditional Jewish enterprises has been promoted by their settlement in Jewish neighborhoods. They get help from fellow refugees, too. In fact, co-ethnic cooperation in business networks has resulted in Los Angeles' Soviet Jews becoming one the most extensively self employed ethnic groups in the United States. Given their short tenure in the U.S., the economic adaptation of Soviet Jews to the United States is impressive indeed.

4

JEWISH IDENTITY AND BEHAVIOR

SITUATIONAL ETHNICITY

When numbers of Soviet Jews began to enter the United States in the late 1970s, many American Jews were overjoyed by the prospect of welcoming their co-religionists. The following quote from a Jewish communal publication celebrated the spirit: "these new Americans, in the near future, should become vital, responsible, and contributing members of our Jewish community." (Schwartz 1980:55). Most emigres also looked forward to joining together with their American cousins on the basis of their common ethnicity and faith. What American and Russian Jews soon learned, however, was that despite their common religious and ethnic persuasion, the expression of their Jewish identity was often drastically different, and reflected the two groups' disparate experiences, values and ways of life. The process Soviet Jews encountered as they sought to express their ethnic identity in America is best understood through the concept of situational ethnicity.

Prior to the 1960s, ethnicity was generally regarded as a fixed and externally defined feature about a person or group. Scholars asserted that ethnicity was based on primordial characteristics such as race, religion, nationality, or family background. While people might occasionally change their name or religion, ethnicity was seen as largely permanent and unchanging. In contrast, recent reports interpret ethnicity as situational in character (Lyman 1977; Nielsen 1985; Nagel 1986; Calhoun 1994). This means that an ethnic identity is not static, but must be actively expressed and made meaningful in any given setting. Definitions of ethnicity often change over time and place. For example, only 100 years ago, Jews, Italians and Irish in American society were considered to be distinct races whereas now they are seen as part of the white majority (Dinnerstein et al. 1990). The frequent shift in the terms applied to American ethnic/racial groups such as colored, Negro, Black, African-American and African; Spanish-American, Hispanic, Latino; and WASP, White, Euro-American and Anglo suggest the ongoing re-definition of ethnicity in American society.

The notion of situational ethnicity was exemplified in the experience of a former student of mine. Darcy, who was a blonde, blue-eyed Chicana (a woman of Mexican-American origins) asserted that she could not rely on her appearance alone to demonstrate her group membership. Describing her cool reception at a summer program for minority students, Darcy explained that she was only accepted as one of the crowd (and not as a token White) after exhibiting her fluency with the vernacular speech of barrio youth. And while Darcy had to prove the Latin-American ancestry that was rightfully hers, several Asian Indian friends report that they are consistently mistaken for Latinos in public settings and that their inability to respond to greetings in Spanish is sometimes taken as an insult by the persons who have erroneously identified them as co-ethnics. Finally, Asian Americans have long encountered incorrect assumptions about their national origins. Following the Pearl Harbor attack, Chinese-Americans often wore badges imprinted with the words "I am Chinese" in an attempt to escape the hostility directed towards Japanese-Americans (Lyman 1975). These several examples show that just because a person is a member of an ethnic group, it does not always follow that the person's ethnic identity will be recognized, and furthermore, that the meaning of ethnicity is not consistent in all settings.

An understanding of the situational determination of ethnicity is a valuable tool for appreciating the ways by which Russian Jewish immigrants must re-establish the meaning of their group membership in the American context. In the former Soviet Union, there was little question about their identity. They knew that they were Jews and so did most of the non-Jews they encountered in their daily lives. Their ethnic identity was maintained by external forces such as the official designation of their nationality as Jewish in their passports, their surnames, their dark-haired Mediterranean appearance in a sea of Slavic blondes, and all too often, by the anti-Semitism they encountered as part of daily life. While Russian Jews also recalled positive aspects of their Jewish identity—foods, songs, stories, feelings of connection with other Jews—a major part of their identity as Jews was negative and imposed on them from the outside. So powerful were the negative implications of their being stigmatized as Jews, in fact, that many Soviet Jews developed means of escaping from their Jewish identity and passing as Russians. Strategies included changing their names to non-Jewish ones, marrying Gentiles and forgoing the circumcision of male children.

The major challenge for Jews in the former Soviet Union was to build up a positive image of themselves in a society that was anti-religious, anti-Semitic and denied Jews the opportunity to learn about themselves, practice their religion or communicate with co-religionists in other nations. One of the great ironies of the experience of Soviet Jews is that although they are victims of ethnic oppression, they are highly assimilated to Soviet society and generally know little about the Jewish religion, Jewish culture or Jewish history. According to historian Arcadius Kahan (1986: 189), as a consequence of Soviet policy, Jews' "identity was stripped of religious, cultural, social, and ethical attributes, and was left only as a mythical, almost mystical quality." In the words of a resettlement worker who is also a Jewish refugee from Eastern Europe: "They may tell you they were proud of being Jewish. I personally don't believe it. Because there was nothing to be proud of. No idea of what there is about being a Jew to be proud, besides that the group is educated or something like this. They do not know their Jewish history, do not know their Jewish tradition." A fairly common strategy through which Soviet Jews worked to develop a positive self image was by emphasizing the biological and inherited nature of their Jewish identity.

Upon entering the U.S., however, Soviet Jews find the ways through which they previously defined themselves as Jews to be suddenly inadequate. In the American context, Soviet Jews encounter relatively little external reinforcement of their group membership. And because of their origins in an atheistic society, they lack the knowledge and record of religious participation that ties American Jews to their community. The reality of being Jewish in the former Soviet Union—shaped by anti-Semitic treatment and emphasis on Jewish inheritance—must be supplanted by an American approach, rooted in a more diverse, pluralistic society and maintained via regular involvement in organized, ethno-religious activities.

Biological Identity in the Former Soviet Union

Because they lacked access to religious training, Russian Jews often emphasized the biological nature of their Jewish identity—associated with body type, appearance, social orientation—a genetic heritage, not a cultural one. For example, in response to questions about what it meant to be Jewish, none of these Jewish immigrants mentioned belief in God. Instead, they were concerned with matters such as the prohibitions and taboos of Judaism, distinguishing between Jewish and non-Jewish characteristics, definitional matters (who is a Jew?) and the numbers and viability of Jews as a racial group. Rooted in biological commonalities, this formulation of Jewish identity allowed Soviet Jews to share in the accomplishments of co-religionists—from Einstein to Chagall, Disraeli and the citizens of Israel, as well as drawing attention to the bond between themselves and the many Soviet heroes rumored to be of Jewish extraction: Karl Marx, several famous

Politburo members and scientists, and Vladimir Vysotsky, the half-Jewish Soviet "Bob Dylan." Finally, by focussing on Judaism as a biological inheritance and a nationality (the way it was officially defined in the Soviet Union) rather than a religious affiliation, Soviet Jews need not feel defensive about their lack of religious knowledge.

Consideration of Judaism as a nationality included dietary restrictions, awareness of Jewish holidays and the display of religious paraphernalia. While few emigres spoke Yiddish and almost none Hebrew, they held these languages in high esteem. The genetic component was also critical in the construction of their identity. Stereotypical Jewish physical characteristics, such as dark, curly hair were considered to be superior to those of fair Russians who were frequently described as alcoholics. Contrary to scientific evidence and the beliefs of U.S. Jews, these biologically-defined Jews seemed to want to believe that they beLong to a separate Jewish race. "Jews have the culture, it is in our blood. Jews have something in the head."

The most enthusiastic advocates of biological Judaism were in their late 50's. Age is an important factor in the development of their perspective. Older individuals did not emphasize this type of identification because they grew up in a period when traditional Jewish training was more available in the USSR (Simon and Simon 1982:34). They often found it easier to identify with more traditional, organized notions of Judaism upon arrival in the States. Younger emigres seldom express this outlook because they rapidly learned American approaches to ethnicity.

As a philosophy, biological Judaism served as a moral sword which Soviet Jews used to resist the twin sources of their oppression: Russian anti-Semitism and Soviet communism. While Soviet communism preached atheism, biological Judaism is rooted in religion (even if its adherents are not religious). While communism is based upon rationalism and modernism, biological Judaism places primacy on belief and sacred tradition. While Soviet communism cultivated universalism and equality, known to be false by the Jewish victims of Soviet anti-Semitism, biological Judaism rejoices in particularism: Jews are the chosen people, different from all others.

While Soviet communism was deeply invested in the love of the Russian motherland, Jews, at least symbolically, love another motherland—Israel—which was the official enemy of the former Soviet Union. Interestingly, many Russian Jews seem to have defined themselves in contrast to the Soviet ideal. Whereas Soviet communism idealizes the hearty, blonde, nationalistic and passionate Russian peasant-worker as model personality, biological Judaism glorifies the slight, worrisome, dark-haired and cosmopolitan scholar. It is clear that this identity is derived, in part, from the anti-Semitic definition of a Jew as "refined, clever, sickly, pampered, finicky, weak, greedy, cunning, cowardly. " (Navrzov 1994:12).

Soviet Jews who sustained biological definitions of their identity were especially concerned with maintaining ethnic boundaries between themselves and non-Jews. They often referred to non-Jewish citizens of the former Soviet Union as Goys (gentiles) or Chazars (pigs). This kind of terminology was uncommon among emigres who did not see their Jewish identity as primarily biological. When I asked Bella Wiseman if she wanted to meet American Jews, she replied "Jewish people, not-Jewish people, just good people!" In contrast, an emigre physicist who focussed on the biological roots of Jewishness described her feelings towards Jews who marry Gentiles: "In Russia, a lot of Jewish people even want their kids to be married to not-Jewish so their grandkids won't have this anti-Semitism problem. But I would hate this for me. Now even here, I wouldn't like my kids to marry non-Jews."

A concrete (as opposed to religious and communal) notion of Judaism appeals to emigres for a number of reasons. First, because they experience guilt over not having gone to Israel, bad feelings are lessened by taking on a "radically Jewish" outlook in the U.S. For example, despite his minimal interest in religion or Zionism (advocacy of Israel), Louis Wiseman would often express his desire to become a commando in the Israel Defense Forces. Second, growing up in an atheistic environment, many emigres have difficulty in adopting religious or spiritual sentiments and values. By developing an outlook that stresses inheritance rather than belief or group involvement as central to Jewish identity, they can assert loyalty without having to confront their ambivalent feelings about religious doctrines and practices (Adorno, et al. 1950). Finally, biological Jews' testimonials about defending the Jewish life against its enemies bear a marked similarity to Soviet calls to protect the Russian homeland and communism against hostile opponents. As former Soviets, they are familiar with these ways of expressing loyalty and group identification.

Because these emigres invented much of their Jewish identity in private and without formal connections to other Jews, they emphasized the reproductive family connection as the most important social link. This is because it is through reproduction that Jewishness is passed from one generation to the next. The family is also the locus of biological Jewish identity because it is the one social institution in Soviet society most able to escape the influence of official ideologies. Based upon this position, biologically-defined Jews frequently accentuated the uniqueness which the possession of this trait implies about themselves and their relatives, rather than the bonds with world Jewry its ownership might suggest. An emigre couple describe what they feel to be their unique status among Soviet Jews: "From my earliest age, I knew I am Jewish. I am proud because of that. It's not so typical for Jewish people from Leningrad or Odessa or Kiev. They feel more Russian. Most Russian Jews are not concerned with this, especially from Moscow or Odessa. They just don't care."

Their inheritance-based approach to Jewishness reveals these emigres' strong desire to connect with their Jewish heritage. Even though they have been unable participate in the kind of activities and learning experiences through which Jews normally acquire a sense of self, they have nevertheless developed an intensely Jewish perspective. More than other emigres, these biological Jews seem both proud of their origins but also angry and bitter about the mistreatment that they, as Jews, have suffered. Their development of this outlook is consistent with other ingenious ways through which Jews in the former Soviet Union were able survive physically, mentally and spiritually in a restrictive and often hostile environment. It is also similar to various "identity politics" movements—Afrocentrism, La Raza—developed by oppressed people who are constantly faced with the larger society's negative stereotypes. Social critic Todd Gitlin describes the appeal of this approach: "Identity politics presents itself as .. the most compelling remedy for anonymity in an otherwise impersonal world" (Gitlin 1994: 153; Calhoun 1994).

Biological Judaism Out of Context

In America, the biological definition of Judaism ceases to be a viable approach to maintaining group identification. Compared to the former Soviet Union, American society is much less aware of or concerned with the existence of Jews as an ethnic group. So, for the Soviet Jews who lack a solid grounding in the Jewish faith, the more distinguishing factors, to other Americans, are their Russian language and traditions. Referring to emigres' loss of the Jewish identity in the U.S., a San Francisco physician commented: "Actually, we do have a joke in the community: 'You have to come to America to become Russian.'"

Consequently, upon arrival in the States, the fact that they are Jews, becomes less clear to those around them. And because identity is a reciprocal process, when others question the emigres' identity, they too become uncertain as to who they are and where they fit in. Finally, as social outsiders, their ability to identify people with whom they come into contact is limited. In interviews, emigres frequently asserted that American Jews seemed indistinguishable from other Americans, and often expressed greater feeling of closeness with non-Jewish immigrants than with native-born Jews.

While there are many negative elements associated with being treated as a minority group, hostility also plays an important role in maintaining in-group identity and solidarity. Following this line of reasoning, sociologists have argued that the recent conflicts experienced by Korean-American shop owners in inner-city neighborhoods have served to unify their community: "A series of conflicts with black customers and other interest groups have made Korean store owners aware of their potential collective threat in this country. This has contributed to the fostering of Korean ethnic solidarity" (Min 1994: 215). Speaking specifically about Jews, French sociologist Emile Durkheim made a similar point, "Indeed, the reproach to which Jews have so long been exposed by Christianity has created feelings of unusual solidarity among them" (1951: 160). However, in contemporary America, Jews encounter few forms of hostile treatment of the type that would set them off from the rest of society. In fact, Jews have been so widely accepted (nearly one in two Jews now marries a Christian) that pundits predict "the ultimate inability of the American Jewish community to survive because they foresee the total assimilation and disappearance of large segments of the American Jewish population into the larger American society and culture" (Waxman 1990: 73).

While the larger society is unlikely to identify Soviet emigres as Jews, neither do their American co-religionists consider them to be more than nominally Jewish at best. American Jews, especially those most active in the Jewish community, expect fellow Jews to be well educated regarding Jewish history and the Jewish religion, to have partaken of various Jewish rituals such as a Bar Mitzvah and a Jewish wedding, to attend a synagogue and to participate in secular Jewish activities, like community centers, clubs, camps and fund-raising campaigns. So accepted are these behaviors as indicators of Jewishness that the American Jewish community regularly measures its well being through surveys which appraise American Jews' involvements in them (Horowitz 1993).

Because recently arrived Jewish immigrants are not familiar with these American forms of displaying Jewishness, they encounter difficulty in demonstrating their identity as Jews to American co-religionists. Further, even though American Jewish communities have developed out-reach programs, emigres often have a hard time participating because they represent a cultural context so different from their prior experience. As a result, Jews from the former Soviet Union who retain their Soviet-based notions of Jewishness in the U.S. encounter isolation and frustration. Marina, a physician who has worked hard to recognize herself as a Jew in the United States, refers to fellow emigres who seem unable to shake their Soviet identities: "Some Russians change countries, but they still live according to rules like in Russia. They leave the country, they use different money, but it takes more than that to realize what is going on here." Emigres who emphasize the biological basis of their Jewish identity would seemingly welcome connection with fellow Jews. Many of their outlooks, such as a strong notion of Jewish identity, a rejection of intermarriage and a desire to support Israel, are quite compatible with those expressed in the larger Jewish community. However, few seemed to actively pursue involvements with either other emigres or American Jews. For example, none of the emigres who expressed this inheritance-based position attended religious services on a regular basis. In fact, one of the families was planning to withdraw their children from Jewish parochial school.

With time, Russian Jews customarily learn to understand American definitions of ethnic membership in general and Judaism in particular. Their young children, growing up with organized religion, have the potential to lead their parents from self-made notions of ethnic and religious identity into more conventional and widely-accepted belief systems. Further, the growth of Russian-oriented Jewish activities—like the Chabad program described in the introduction—offer a context much more compatible with the Russian roots of their religious identities. Among the established emigre population, many patterns of identification are now observable. Their religious involvements range from orthodoxy to secular Judaism and even occasional conversions to Christianity. Realizing their strong connections to the country of origin, many Jews from the former Soviet Union also include a major component of Russianness as part of their identity as well.

Finally, as the following comment suggests, perhaps some Soviet Jews will immigrate to Israel, where they hope the absence of non-Jews will allow them to resolve their dilemmas about Jewish identity. "It was my main driving point to move to Israel for my kids not to solve these (Jewish identity) problems ever. What you have to do, what you don't have to do, are you Jewish and what you have to do to be Jewish. Living in Israel, you don't have to worry about this."

In fact, few emigres move to Israel or join Orthodox movements in order to limit contact with non-Jews. Rather, over time, the majority develop the knowledge, skills and resources they need to understand the meaning of their ethnicity—in terms of its many components—in the American setting. The following paragraphs describe Soviet Jews' Americanized perspectives on their identity.

JEWISH IDENTITY AND BEHAVIOR IN THE UNITED STATES

As the discussion of biological Judaism indicates, Jewish identity is a complex issue for Soviet emigres. While only 4 percent of emigres in a nationwide survey claimed to have had one year of Jewish education prior to migration, at the same time, many have deep feelings about being Jewish and a strong ethnic or national identification as Jews and Russians (Kosmin 1990: 39; Markowitz 1993).

Nearly all of the emigres I spoke to are interested in exploring their connections to Judaism. Further, coming from a society where religion was all but banned, many are curious about investigating this forbidden ideology—along with others such as psychology, EST and Eastern religions. Finally, as social outsiders, emigres are attracted to the idea of joining a warm and supportive American Jewish community. However, because religion was so unfamiliar, relatively few emigres develop extensive involvements in American Jewish activities, and fewer still become explicitly religious. For the most part, Jewish identification among emigres is secular or nationalistic rather than religious. In his country-wide survey of Jews from the former USSR, Kosmin (1990: 35) found that over 60 percent of emigre respondents felt that the meaning of being Jewish in America was "cultural" or "a nationality," while less than 30 percent felt it was "religious." A San Francisco area emigre activist spoke about the contrasting notions of Jewish identity among Soviet emigres and American Jews: "I want the American community to understand who we are. First of all, we are not like your grandparents, people from Sholem Aleichem [the author of traditional Eastern European Jewish stories]. We are educated, professional people. The community in general, it's non-religious and that's it. Because we don't have religious ground, (we) have to form this ground first, but I don't think this will be an overnight thing." Some emigres had cynical responses to my questions concerning Jewish involvement. When I asked Svetlanna about her views, she described a cousin who had attended a Jewish high school: "She's very religious. When it's Saturday, she won't drive. In that school, they just totally propagandize her. But she doesn't have values—she's more crooked than anything I've seen. In my opinion, sending her there was a waste of money."

Few respondents were as actively hostile to religion as Svetlanna. Several described their initial desire to become more immersed in a religious life, but said they ultimately found religious rituals to be lacking in meaning and moral relevance. Paulina, for example, explained why she abandoned efforts to build upon what her children learned in the temple that had hosted her family. "When we came here, I tried to celebrate [Jewish] holidays. My kids know all the songs, we did all the stuff. But not very seriously, because we don't understand." Like many emigres, she retained some elements of Russian-style Jewish identity, claiming that religion and spiritual issues were personal and internal—they reside "in the heart" and are not readily connected to formal religious participation. "Americans say that they know religion and we Russians do not. I am not sure who is really more religious. Religion is something inside. This is why I don't think all this religious training is important for my kids. I want them to grow up like good people and be good inside. We're not religious people okay, but we have another Torah. [The body of Jewish religious literature]. We have something like our own commandments."

While fewer in number than the secular majority, various emigres have become religious Jews in the U.S.; some as members of Chabad or other Orthodox movements, others in mainstream American temples (Freedman 1993; Gorbis 1992; Ruby 1993). Because religion offers a means of affiliation to American society, emigres like Mary Kogan consciously worked to involve their families in the American synagogue that sponsored their resettlement. Admitting that religious ceremonies were alien to her way of thinking, Mary nevertheless asserted "It might not be important for American Jews who are not religious, but you have your connections, you have your friends. But for people like us who are just coming in, it is very important to have some connections. I have some friends from Lvov. They are not into religion, but they went to the synagogue and said: 'We grow up in an atheistic country but we are Jews and we would like to participate, even if we are not religious.' And they got friends, and they got connections are they are quite happy."

Several surveys indicate that once they are settled, Jews from the former USSR belong to synagogues at about the same rate as native-born Jews—about 40 percent (Kosmin 1990). In the words of Azary, an engineer from Moscow, living in Oakland: "I am a modern Jew, but when I went to the Shabbat [Sabbath] dinner sponsored by our synagogue, it was the first time I ever felt like a Jew. We live near the synagogue and we go every week. We eat Kosher food. My son will get a Bar Mitzvah. American Jews can learn Hebrew, so we can talk to Jews all over the world. All of this is very good." Markowitz (1991: 23) concludes in her study of emigre teenagers in Chicago, that considering their lack of Jewish education and confrontations with anti-Semitism, Soviet Jews' religious leanings should be taken as a cup half full: "What is remarkable here is not that these young women have decided not to escape their Jewishness but that they have increased their Jewish activities and turned a stigmatized identity into a positive one."

The Ethnic Dimension

A unique aspect of Jewish identity is that it involves both religious and ethnic components. There is a long tradition of secular Jews who do not conform to religious teachings, but express their Jewish identity through food, language, music, literature, social ties, humor and place of residence. These ways of maintaining a secular or ethnic Jewish identification often appeal to emigres. Despite low levels of religious education, Soviet Jews are in many ways more "ethnic" than American Jews in terms of their involvement with co-ethnic persons, networks and outlooks. Sociologist Herbert Gans

(1979) describes assimilated, American Jews who have lived in the States for three or four generations as maintaining "symbolic ethnicity." That is, they connect with their heritage by choice, through identity-related, expressive behaviors and rituals. In other words, while these Jews speak perfect English and interact flawlessly in American society, they may listen to Klezmer music, visit Israel, eat deli food, or season their language with Yiddish expressions when the mood strikes them. This contrasts with the more extensive reliance on ethnic communities, forms of communication, and social patterns maintained by first generation groups, such as the Soviets.

Soviet emigres' strong ethnic ties come out in their responses to several questions in the 1990-91 New York Jewish Population Study. Jews from the former Soviet Union have higher rates of Yiddish competence, membership in JCCs (Jewish Community Centers) and YMHAs (Young Men's and Women's Hebrew Associations) and reading Jewish publications than all New York Jews. They are much more likely to have close friends or immediate family living in Israel than all New York Jews, exceed all New York Jews by 30 percent in agreeing with the statement that most or all of their closest friends are Jewish; and much more strongly believe that when it comes to a crisis, Jews can only depend on other Jews. Jews from the former USSR also have more negative views of Jewish-Gentile intermarriage, even when the non-Jewish spouse converts to Judaism, than do all New York Jews (Gold 1994).

POTENTIAL FOR AMALGAMATION WITHIN THE AMERICAN JEWISH COMMUNITY

American Jews' initial hopes that the Soviets would quickly join their religious community may have been unrealistically optimistic, but cynics who see no potential for involvement with American Jews are also misinformed. Although emigres may resent aspects of their resettlement program and sometimes dissociate themselves from American Jewish values, many have tried to connect with the American Jewish community. They have joined synagogues, sent their children to Jewish day schools and camps, participated in Jewish community activities, and contributed funds to Jewish philanthropies. Emigres live in Jewish neighborhoods, are often employed in traditionally Jewish occupations, decorate their homes and offices with Judaica, and have levels of ethnic attachment that exceed those of native born Jews.

Other common characteristics may provide bases for future cooperation. Both Russian and American Jews are largely secular, have high levels of intermarriage with Gentiles, value academic achievement, and are heavily concerned with the advancement of their children (Gold 1994; Lipset 1990). National survey data indicate that Russian emigres' affiliation with organized religious life is not too different from that of American Jews: The rank order of Soviet emigres' denominational membership—Reform, then Conservative, Orthodox and Reconstructionist—as well as their rate of synagogue membership is the same as that of the larger community. However, in Los Angeles, emigres are most heavily involved in Chabad—a unique form of Orthodox Judaism (Krautman 1990)]. According to the New York Jewish Population Study 1990-91, 57 percent of emigres in New York gave gifts to Jewish charities in the year prior to the survey. While their gifts were admittedly smaller, this number was only 9 percent less than that of all Jewish New Yorkers (Gold 1994).

One way of assessing the future connection of emigres to American Jewish life is to consider the extent to which their children are becoming socialized into American Judaism through a Jewish education. Surveys and fieldwork reflect a strong but conditional interest on the part of emigre parents in promoting their children's participation in Jewish activities. When free or reduced Jewish day-school tuition was offered to recently arrived Soviet emigre children, a large portion accepted, although as fee waivers expired, many left these schools (Federation 1985; Barber 1987). Emigre parents often send their children to Jewish schools for non-religious reasons; they dislike the lack of safety, attention, and discipline associated with urban public schools. Not unlike most American Jews, the Soviets generally favor academic over religious training and frequently object to expending more than what they consider to be a minimal amount of time on religious studies. As Paulina said, "This year, we don't go to synagogue because last year, the kids went four times per week. It's too much. We decided this year to take a break. Maybe next year, we'll start again." Finally, some emigres, like Lilly who removed her kids from a San Francisco Hebrew Academy, reject religious schools because they believe in pluralism: "That's what I explained to Rabbi Lichtenstein. I want my kids not in Hebrew school, not in Catholic school but just a normal public school. They should get along with the different people. Now, while the kids are young, they should learn about other people."

Despite these objections to religious education, one study found that 80 percent of emigre 12-year-olds' parents sent them to some kind of Jewish education (Kosmin 1990: 39). Again, as is the case for many American Jews, Jewish education attendance is most directly associated with preparation for the Bar or Bat Mitzvah (the ritual celebrating a young Jew's religious coming-of-age), with participation falling off rapidly after completing the ceremony at age 13.

CONCLUSION

Soviet Jews come to the U.S. with very different interpretations of their ethnic and religious identity than those maintained by their American co-religionists. The difficulty experienced by Soviet Jews in expressing their identity in the United States, coupled with American Jews' lack of insight into their patterns of ethnic identification, makes a strong case for understanding the situational basis of ethnicity—and not just as a sociological concept—but rather, as tool for dealing with real people. On the other hand, the primordialist assumption that Jews everywhere can understand each other simply because they are all Jews is found to be lacking as we consider the problems involved in the ethnic and religious adaptation of Soviet Jews. Despite initial difficulties, with time, emigres do make progress in developing a collectively-based identity which has meaning on American soil. While most Soviet Jews are not religious, they do maintain a level of ethnic attachment to their community that is more intense than that of American Jews. In addition, a growing number are participating in forms of Jewish life that they find personally meaningful. And because many have relatives and friends in Israel, they tend to have close ties to the Jewish State.

In the future, ethnic communities need to realize that their subgroups are likely to have very different ways of establishing connections and showing who they are, reflecting their unique circumstances, values and environments. By considering the potential for diversity and the contextual basis of ethnic identity, the possibility for smooth and inclusive interactions among diverse subgroups might be increased.

5

COMMUNITY FORMATION AMONG JEWS FROM THE FORMER SOVIET UNION

PERSPECTIVES ON THE EMIGRE COMMUNITY

Given their numbers and unique patterns of adaptation, it is surprising that Soviet Jews have failed to capture much attention from the mass media, academics, or the general public. So far, few resources have been devoted to assessing this group's collective adjustment to the United States. One reason Soviet Jewish immigrants have not attracted more attention is that they are highly educated—and white. Because they blend into the majority community, Soviets do not remind the American public of the country's changing ethnic composition or of foreign powers who seem to threaten our security or economic well being. They have not been associated with social problems. Nor are they singled out as the "model minority" successes like some recent Asian groups. Although articles, TV news segments, and a recent movie portray the existence of "A Russian mafia" in the U.S., the public seems indifferent about adding Russians to the canon of ethnic criminals celebrated in tabloids and action films.

In contrast to the highly visible ethnic businesses in Orange County's Little Saigon, Los Angeles' Koreatown, or Miami's Little Havana, the Russian-Jewish presence is far less apparent. Many emigres are self employed but only a few post Cyrillic signs. All in all, these cold war refugees have joined American society with surprisingly little notice.

Perhaps resettlement agencies have intentionally kept their Soviet emigre clients out of the limelight. They have been wary of documentation and research because broad statements regarding either a triumphant or troubled pattern of adaptation could yield negative results: too much success might justify reductions in funding, while too little would provoke criticism of agencies and a cutback in the number Jews from the former USSR permitted to enter the country as refugees (Gold 1994). Because the very settlement of Soviet Jews in the United States rather than Israel is a subject of controversy in the Jewish community, conflicts might be avoided by limiting public declarations about the group.

Models of Adaptation: Jewish Assimilation and Ethnic Associations

Soviet Jews have received little discussion, too, because their unique and unanticipated pattern of adaptation is a source of potential embarrassment to the two expert groups—Jewish agencies involved in resettling Soviet Jews, and scholars of immigration—who failed to predict it.

The initial (and ongoing) hope of the American Jewish community was that Soviet Jews would be passionately interested in living a Jewish life and would quickly join the American Jewish community. According to an authority on the Soviet Jewish emigration: "A motivating force in this community's commitment to help resettle the Soviet Jews was its hope that they would develop a strong Jewish identity, that they would participate in American Jewish communal life, and that their children would become part of the American Jewish scene" (Simon 1985: 31). For the reasons discussed in the previous chapter, this integration into the American Jewish community has not occurred, at least not in the way that the American community had envisioned (Gold 1994; Carp 1990; Barber 1987; Markowitz 1993).

If American Jews predicted that Soviet refugees would join their communities, academic specialists thought that the emigres would inevitably develop ethnic solidarity through the formation of their own strong ethnic associations. Drawing from the experience of successful ethnic groups like turn-of-the-century Jews, Asians and Cubans, scholars of immigration have developed a widely influential model of immigrant adaptation which emphasizes the positive effect of joining formal ethnic associations. For example, Cuban and Korean trade associations have assisted large numbers of newcomers in finding jobs within their immigrant communities. Family, or hometown organizations such as the contemporary Vietnam Chinese Mutual Aid and Friendship Association and the pre-World War II organizations, the Jewish Landsmanschaften and Japanese Kenjinkai, were established to provide direction, support and a social life to those recently arrived from overseas (Light 1972; Gold 1992). Scholars assert that these types of associations provide immigrant groups with social stability, moral guidance and economic support, even in hostile environments: ethnic communities represent an ideal form of collective life, maintaining "an inclusive whole, celebrating the interdependence of public and private life and the different callings of all" (Bellah, et al. 1985: 72-73; Glazer and Moynihan 1963; Portes and Rumbaut 1990).

Because educated, contemporary immigrants generally conform to this model and Jews are particularly noteworthy for their organizational proclivity and communal concern, such theories would predict that the new Soviet Jewish immigrants would form similar organizations to facilitate adaptation to life in the U.S. (Hyfler 1991). This has not been the case. Indeed, following her intensive fieldwork in America's largest Soviet Jewish settlement, Fran Markowitz has described this paucity of ethnic associations in an essay entitled "Community without Organizations" (Markowitz 1992).

AMBIVALENCE ABOUT SOCIAL MEMBERSHIP

While the Soviet Jewish enclave is united by language, immigration experience, networks of sponsorship, social bonds among the elderly, political outlook, estrangement from American Jews, and shared notions of ethnic identity, it is also segmented. Feelings of distrust and individualism are pervasive within the community, causing many emigres to distance themselves from co-ethnics. Emigres frequently described one another with indignation and questioned their peers' moral integrity. In interviews, emigres of all social stripes made statements that depicted fellow Russians in the most suspicious fashion: "Seven out of 10 Russians that I know are into something illegal. They are either smuggling this or they're avoiding tax—a lot of them are going to jail." Or, "A lot of Russian women have American lovers, and their husbands know. Nothing is done about it." And "See, they think that they're so smart, and that Americans are just stupid and they can lie and cheat and no one will ever know. You can do it for a certain amount of time, but once you get caught, that's it."

Emigres frequently claimed that their fellows came to the United States, not as religious refugees or even anti-Communists but rather, as financially motivated immigrants. A mathematician from St. Petersburg commented: "If they tell you about religion, don't believe them. Russian Jews don't know anything about religion. They just came over here because they heard that it is easy to get a car. None of them attend synagogue." Even well known Russian Chabad Rabbis who obtained significant contributions were often described as "businessmen" by community members.

While emigres disapproved of some American social mores—what they say are Americans' shallow ways of interacting and making friends—they often appreciated Americans' civility, optimism, and cooperation. Many complained when fellow former Soviets, especially members of the recently arrived "second wave" migration, acted in what they felt was a typically Russian fashion. Emigres frequently described being offended when they first realized that the common American salutation "How are you?" is simply a greeting rather than a serious inquiry into another person's well being. Having learned this social rule the hard way, Russians treat this ritual as a general indicator of Americans' superficial approach to human relationships. However, after being subjected to her recently arrived boyfriend's typically Russian brooding, Mila has come to believe that the American way is really better. She explains: "Here, when they ask 'How are you?', you're just supposed to say 'Oh, everything is fine'. But my boyfriend, he would say 'The reality is that nothing is fine'. To me it seems like the American way is better because the more you keep telling pessimistic and depressing stuff to yourself, psychologically, the more you're going to believe it. He complains about everything. Nothing and no one is right. He doesn't like anyone—everyone's got a problem. He knows everything; he doesn't need anyone to tell him, you know. They're all like that. They all think they know everything."

Emigres commonly described community events with embarrassment and revulsion. One man went so far as to claim that he avoided speaking Russian in public, lest he be associated with other emigres. An unemployed engineer denounced his co-ethnics as he described the behavior of Soviet Jews at the showing of a Russian movie in San Francisco: "The movie was sold out, so some people tried to crash the door, pushing and shoving. I was disgusted. I went to a parade on Market Street—300,000 Americans. The people got along fine. Everyone was happy and smiling. But only a few hundred of Russians get together at a movie and everyone is fighting already."

With this kind of outlook pervasive in the community, it is especially hard for emigres to use their many common concerns and values as a basis for organization. As Mila pointed out "That's one thing about Russians. A lot of them are leaders. They don't like to be followers. I'm like that too. I'm a total leader and I can't stand following."

Also working against community organization is that Soviet Jews come from a diversity of occupational, regional and cultural origins in the USSR (Gitelman 1978). They may feel little interest in or attachment to the mass of Soviet Jews in the United States. Loss of rank complicates matters. Many feel ashamed when confronted by their countrymen because they have experienced downward occupational mobility in the United States. Others are unwilling to join with people they regard as having inferior backgrounds. Several people complained that being associated with a mass of uncouth emigres with whom they had no connection in the USSR was unnatural and humiliating. An emigre who now works as an insurance salesman describes his ambivalence towards other Soviet Jews: "In Russia, I was highly educated. I had highly educated friends. I never used to be in the company of haircutters. It wasn't because I didn't like them. They just wasn't to my level. Now we are all together. You see it different times at this table: people who drive the taxi and who make manicures, a lot of different people. The life mix all kind of people, so you can't stay alone. You can't stay from them."

Regionalism is also a source of division. Generally, emigres from Russia (especially Moscow and St. Petersburg) feel themselves to be above those from the Ukraine. Among immigrants from the Ukraine, those from Kiev sometimes denigrate Odessans. A woman born in Bobruysk, Belarus spoke of some regional stereotypes held by emigres: "The people from my city, they say are crooks. The people from Odessa, they say are two-faced. They always smile and tell you that you look nice and then they'll turn around and totally give you the evil eye. And then, people from Kiev are supposed to be brutes and rude. Moldavians—they're supposed to be the stupidest people in the world. No brains. They just scratch their heads. Moscow and Leningrad—snotty and very diplomatic."

Clearly, the divisions I've mentioned and ambivalent feelings towards fellow refugees help explain the small number of formal organization among Soviet Jews that has been noted in California and New York (Gold 1992; Markowitz 1992; Gorbis 1992). Another important factor is the legacy of forced collectivism. Not only are Soviet Jews averse to joining any formal organizations, they also have a negative attitude toward the activists who try to get them to do so. Many emigres assume that persons who take leadership roles in communal activities do so only in order to obtain some personal benefit. According to a report on Soviet Jewish emigre organizations, emigres have "developed a very strong negative attitude toward such organizations and activities" and "the figure of the social activist acquired a permanent negative classification in the minds of many new immigrants" (Ilyin and Kagan 1991:5). An emigre describes this position: "Russian Jewish for generations were under the pressure of communism and they are tired of the different organizations. Here, Russian Jewish—they want to be free from all organization, because there is no freedom in Russia this way." Unfortunately, this attitude also interferes with the development new ethnic associations in the U.S. In the words of one man, "You try to get together. You have 20 people and 20 opinions and no one is really trained to compromise, so it is difficult."

The emigre community also includes few leaders whose status is carried over from the country of origin. Indeed, Communist Party membership is looked down upon here. Further, unlike earlier immigrants who were forced to band together to survive (Howe 1976; Wirth 1928; Light 1972; Glazer and Moynihan 1963; Portes and Rumbaut 1990), Soviet Jews are provided with an efficient battery of resettlement services (Eckles et al. 1982; Gold 1994). Many such services, specifically designed to forge links between Soviet Jewish individuals and entrenched American Jewish institutions communities, may hinder the development of emigre self-help activities (Goldberg 1981; Schiff 1980; Schwartz 1980; Carp 1990). Consequently, by their very existence, resettlement services offer a disincentive to group formation.

Finally, Jews from the former USSR are often able to obtain support, advice, material needs, and a social life through participation in *informal* networks and collectivities (Markowitz 1993). If they get help this way, refugees have less incentive to create, or join, formal organizations.

THE EMIGRE COMMUNITY

Despite the lack of formal organizations, the recent Soviet Jewish immigrants have established an active communal life based on shared language, values, customs and experience.

Jews from the former Soviet Union tend to settle in common areas, often in existing Jewish neighborhoods. These communities of settlement were established when American Jews helped the first wave of emigres find housing. Once a known emigre settlement was established, it became a magnet and more recent arrivals established homes there as well. Indeed, several emigres I met had moved to Los Angeles and San Francisco after being initially placed Jewish agencies in small midwestern or southern communities with few other Russians. Mila lived for several years in the deep South. "My brother and I both, we have Jewish noses and curly, frizzy hair. You know, typical Jewish things. I never fit in. When we first came to L.A., I started meeting all the Russians. And then I totally felt like in my own shoes. I felt comfortable. I mean, I just clicked with them from the beginning, from the very first word."

Soviet Jewish communities have developed in several locations. The largest in the U.S. is in the Brighton Beach area of Brooklyn, New York (Markowitz 1993; Orleck 1989; Littman 1993). In Los Angeles, Soviet Jews have concentrated in West Hollywood, while in San Francisco, the geographical and social center of the Soviet Jewish community is located in the Sunset and Richmond districts. In Massachusetts, emigres have established enclaves in Brighton, Allston, and the North Shore. In Chicago, Soviet Jews assemble in the Devon area of the North Side as well as in Skokie, and in Detroit many reside in suburban Oak Park. I call these areas "Soviet Jewish enclaves." Soviet Jewish enclaves are loose networks of emigres representing a wide variety of occupations, regional origins, degrees of religious identification, and outlooks on adjustment to the U.S.

Interaction among members is frequent. Within the Soviet Jewish enclave, a fairly high level of institutional completeness exists (Breton 1964). For example, in West Hollywood or Brighton Beach, a Soviet Jew can interact with neighbors, shop for food, clothes or appliances, see a doctor or dentist, attend religious services, read a newspaper, watch cable TV, visit a local park to play dominoes, and interact with numerous acquaintances, all without speaking a word of English (Orleck 1987: Markowitz 1993).

Ties to family and friends are an important source of social attachment in the Soviet Jewish enclave. Established emigres sponsor relatives who have recently arrived from the former Soviet Union or other parts of the United States. Within the enclave, a great deal of information is exchanged during frequent social visits. Various publications, notably *Novoye Russkoye Slovo* (New York) and *Panorama* (Los Angeles) are available as well as Russian language TV and radio (Kosmin 1990). Emigres provide each other with services such as child care, auto repair, computer training, music lessons, and investment advice. Because the recently arrived are baffled by the complexities of American economic life, emigres' use of their community connections to obtain information before making major decisions such as looking for work, purchasing expensive items or enrolling in trade school. Social activities take place in the enclave, and mates and companions are often found there. Resettlement services are at hand, and informal community connections reduce the cultural and linguistic problems refugees face when they deal with American service providers (Gold 1987; Goldberg 1981; Dorf and Katlin 1983; Ivry 1993).

A Russian-born attorney writes about the social milieu of the Soviet Jewish community in Los Angeles: "Restaurants, night life, parties, celebrations and invitations to family events give real shape to the community. All are informal groupings based largely on considerations such as location by city or region, age or length of residency in the U.S. Groups such as the Kiev Gang, the *Zapadenski* (Western Ukrainians) and the Odessa Club tend to gravitate together, and develop and validate their own agendas as well" (Gorbis 1992: 20).

Soviet Jewish enclaves have a strong attraction for their residents, who often commute long distances to and from work in order to live among co-ethnics. Despite the general trend for middle class Angelenos to leave urban neighborhoods in the face of rising crime, cutbacks in government services, the 1992 L.A. Riot, and 1994 Northridge Earthquake, Soviet Jews described their plans to remain near the urban center in West Hollywood. Svetlanna, a college student, told me about the unhappy experiences of refugees who left West Hollywood for newer, suburban regions of the Los Angeles area: "They'll come into the city and say 'Oh, why did I move?' My parents [who moved to Los Angeles from Texas] always tell people 'don't move, you're going to come right back'. In the earthquake—some of them got really messed up. And after the riots, they just complained about the neighborhood. They've all got their businesses and where are they gonna go? By the time they decide to move, the riots are over and everything is fine and back to normal. They'll just tough it out."

Friendship and Social Life in the Emigre Community

In coming from the former Soviet Union to California, Soviet Jews encounter major transformations in nearly every area of their lives—ranging from the political system, the economy, and geography to the language, climate, diet and sexual mores. Despite these manifold changes, emigres often focus on the issue of friendship as the single aspect of existence that seems most different in the U.S.

Interviewees as well as the literature describing life in the former Soviet Union emphasize the depth and profundity of friendships in Worker's State. In a society where so much of life was controlled, politicized and regulated, close friendships—along with family relations—were among the only points of contact where a person could really open up and express him or herself fully and spontaneously without fear of repercussions (Shlapentokh 1984).

Emigres point out that Soviet friendships generally took years to develop, as compatriots shared life's joys, challenges and hardships. True friends were desperately and intimately involved with each other. A friend's accomplishments and heartaches were taken as one's own. Even a companion's pets and prized belongings were celebrated: one young emigre from Kiev recounted with pride and nostalgia the meaning of Sasha's record collection and Misha's curios to his relations with these boyhood chums. Lacking the omnipresent distractions provided by a consumer culture's entertainment industry (cable TV, videos,

Nintendo games, multiplex cinemas and the like), Soviet friends had time for long and passionate conversations about politics, music, art and their hopes, dreams and fears. Their relationships were intense and highly developed. Further, because people lived close together and had relatively leisurely schedules, friends saw each other often. A norm of informality and hospitality meant that one's door was always open—companions were unconditionally welcome to drop by at any time.

The grim economic environment of the Soviet system—wherein everything from food to heating oil was in scarce supply—also fostered closeness. Although a Soviet Jew could never count on the availability goods, they could always rely on the companionship of their friends. And whatever goods were at hand would be generously shared. Even in the U.S., where 24 hour supermarkets ensure the constant availability of nourishment, emigres retain the custom of feeding all comers. Never did I visit a Soviet Jewish home, regardless of time of day or night without being offered generous platters of food—bread, meat, soup, cake, wine, fish and tea.

In coming to the U.S., however, the institution of Soviet friendship was forever transformed. Becoming familiar with American life and earning a living in a free-market economy takes a great deal of time and energy—leaving less available for socializing. Further, in California emigres sometimes settle far from one another, making quick visits impossible. Having left the repressive contours of the Soviet Union, emigres no longer need to nurture trusting relations in order to express their political sentiments or opinions of co-workers. And the relative opulence of the U.S. means that the need for sharing scarce goods (as well as the bonds reinforced by their sharing) was no longer a part of life. Prior to migration, a social evening might involve a passionate discussion of poetry late into the night while savoring a prized bottle of vodka or wine. In Los Angeles, on the other hand, less profound topics, like the merits of IBM versus Apple or Volvo versus Toyota, are the likely focus of conversation—(with the kids' MTV blaring in the next room). And while wine is no longer in short supply, one had better not imbibe because the Highway Patrol are out tonight. Besides, work starts at 7 am.

Despite these many challenges, emigres retained the tradition of close friendship, keeping in touch with old friends—in the U.S. and overseas—and making new ones. The affluence of the States offers opportunities for more elaborate celebrations than before. Many of the emigres I knew socialized on weeknights as well as weekends. While some lived in suburbs, many remained in close-packed neighborhoods like San Francisco's Richmond and Sunset Districts and West Hollywood. Emigres also enjoy travel and frequently take weekend trips to Los Vegas, Lake Tahoe or Disneyland, and longer excursions to Hawaii, Europe and Israel, all in the company of family and friends.

Emigres are well aware of the transformation of their social relations, but most felt they could do little to stop it. Herman, an engineer, reflected on American ideas about relationships. "In America, when you know someone for fifteen minutes, they are your friend. For us, this is so totally absurd." An insurance salesman made a similar point. "You can't mix yourself with Americans. A lot of our people try to, but you can't do it. I can spend an hour talking to Americans, but we are different people. It's not because they are bad people or I don't like them. For me, I don't trust them because I don't know where to find this point to trust them or not." Despite these comments, faced with the demands of work, commuting and family, emigres realized that American habits and relationships were becoming their own. They find themselves telephoning before making increasingly less frequent visits. "In America," said Sasha, "you can own so many things. Perhaps you don't need Russian friendships."

Soviet Jews comment on how American housing stock changes their social lives. Single family home ownership has long been a status symbol for immigrant groups in America. However, Soviet Jews, who are used to dwelling in apartments in the densely populated cities of the former Soviet Union, often treat home ownership as a mixed blessing, since apartments allow a much higher level of social involvement with neighbors than do separate homes. Mila, a college student, discussed this as she describes her parents' home in Beverly Hills "I really like our house, but it bothers me that it's like all the way up Laurel Canyon, it's kinda like deserted. There are houses around but it's not like everyone knows each other. I don't know anyone. We never see anyone. And I'm scared to be at home alone." In many cases, Jews from the former Soviet Union combined Russian and California life styles by settling en masse in apartment buildings and condo complexes. In this way, they achieve a combination of personal space and social closeness that they find pleasing.

While emigres often find that they are unable to maintain the quality of social life that they enjoyed in the former USSR, a whole series of commercial establishments have been developed which allow emigres to get together in the States. Emigres meet one another and exchange gossip in the ethnically owned delicatessens, retail stores and beauty shops described in Chapter 3. The most important social institution is the Russian Jewish nightclub. These large nightspots offer a lavish variety of Russian-style food and drink and feature song-and-dance entertainers versed in Russian, Jewish and American popular music. They have become the centers of Soviet Jewish communities throughout the United States. Such settings provide an environment where flashily dressed emigres spend long evenings in celebration of religious and secular events in a style that combines their Russian, Jewish and American identities. "Russian restaurants exemplify to an extreme the core value of hospitality as they provide their patrons with comfort and sensual pleasures to excess. These restaurants are decorated with plush wallpaper, mirrors, flashing lights inlaid in the dance floor, long dining tables draped in linen and covered with china and flowers . . . Women arrive heavily made-up in shiny lipstick and thick, black mascara . . . The restaurants are institutionalized showplaces that bring Soviet emigres together . . . because they provide arenas in which individuals can demonstrate success and measure themselves in terms of their fellow emigres" (Markowitz 1993: 237-8).

In addition to the "restaurant scene," emigres also join together in parks, at the Chabad Russian program and in each others' homes. School aged emigres report that they often hang out in Russian cliques at school. When I visited the San Francisco Jewish Community Center with three young emigres, I was surprised at the number of Russians in attendance. It turns out that they were given free memberships by the by the host community. The JCC's steamroom was especially popular, because spas, saunas and public baths were favorite recreation spots in the former Soviet Union (Smith 1976). Finally, a succession of interest-based clubs revolving around sports, literature, poetry, art and various occupations and professions provides a venue for emigre social life.

Community Links

As suggested by their attachment to the Soviet Jewish enclave and its social life, Jews from the former Soviet Union, especially the great majority from the European Republics, share numerous similarities. They tend to be educated, urbanized, Russian-speaking, and maintain many common values, which are generally more conservative than those of their Jewish and gentile American neighbors.

The elderly provide an important source of affiliation the enclave. And there are many of them. Thirty four percent of Soviet Jews entering the U.S. in 1991 were 50 or older (HIAS 1993: 14). Because aged emigres do not generally become fluent in English and are less likely than younger Soviet Jews to find employment here, they are dependent upon each other for a social life and upon their families for transportation, translation, and other necessities (Simon 1985). Elderly emigres with time on their hands meet each other in agencies, shops, apartment hallways, and synagogues. Here, they establish relationships with other elderly Jews which sometimes unite entire families.

The presence of so many elderly emigres helps keep Soviet Jews in Russian enclaves. The younger adults would often rather move to suburban areas where housing is less expensive but they frequently remain in the Soviet Jewish enclaves because elderly parents want to be near other Russian speakers. From morning until night, West Hollywood's Plummer Park is frequented by elderly emigres—picknicking, playing cards and dominos, strolling with their grand-children, or just making conversation. A similar social environment can be found on the boardwalk in Brighton Beach, Brooklyn (Orleck 1987; Markowitz 1993).

Emigres also stick together because they have difficulty establishing social links with non-emigres. Despite their initial hope that interactions with American Jews would be easy, many emigres discovered that the cultural and linguistic gulf was difficult to cross. "From the beginning," said a Soviet Jew who has lived in the U.S. for ten years, "everybody wants to be assimilated, to get out of this Russian ghetto. But after that, a lot of people had a problem socializing with American Jews. And English is not their language. After a while, they get back together and about 75 percent of the community is completely satisfied with what they have." A similar point was made by college student Mila, regarding her attempts to befriend American Jewish peers. "With them it's not the same. God, I can't talk to them for five minutes and you know it's, 'Get me away.' I just want to go."

Young emigres—even those who seem totally Americanized—reveal their commitment to the Soviet Jewish enclave as they continue to socialize with other Jews from the former USSR despite having lived in the U.S. for years. I interviewed several college students who came to the U.S. prior to age 5, attended American schools, spoke English perfectly, yet still remained extremely close to their parents and socialized almost exclusively within emigre peer groups (see also Markowitz 1991; 1993).

Mila, a college student who has been in the U.S. for 15 years, commented on her social preferences: "The American friends—quote, unquote—that I have are just people that I see in class or on the tennis team. But the on weekends, my real friends are all Russians. It's the same with everyone. It's something in your soul. Like my brother. When he was younger, he's like 'Oh God, I never want to be with Russians.' But lately, he's changed. He only wants to have Russian friends. He even talks about hopefully marrying a Russian girl, you know, who is Americanized but still with the Russian background and culture." This cultural synthesis is the form of adaptation that many find optimal: The ideal is to take advantage of the openness and affluence of American life, its greater sexual freedom, and the opportunity for young people to live in their own apartments or dormitories, but to enjoy these benefits with others steeped in Russian culture.

In their study of dating behavior, Fruchtbaum and Skager found a similar motif. Although the teenage girls they studied have lived in the U.S. for from 8 to 14 years, all "expressed their preference for Russian men as boyfriends and marriage partners." They believed it would be easier to understand, trust, and become close with a young man with whom they shared a common background. The strong Russian-Jewish family influenced mate choice as the girls' parents encouraged them to date Russians. "The need for the boyfriend to be accepted by the parents and the family, and the importance of good communication between parents and the boyfriend were expressed by all of the participants" (Fruchtbaum and Skager 1989: 24).

EMIGRE ORGANIZATIONS

In addition to the informal social community of Russian Jews, there are some organizations that have managed to attract a number of these Russian immigrants. Soviet Jews as well as their American sponsors realize that, regardless of the general resistance to organization, many problems of adaptation could be alleviated by the creation of viable emigre groups. Hence, several emigres have managed to create groups that deal with political issues, while other successful organizations have attracted emigres who share common occupational and religious interests. According to Ilyin and Kagan's national survey of Soviet emigre associations, these groups seek to help newcomers adapt to the U.S., to retain Russian language and culture, and to develop a Jewish identity. They vary widely in terms of their emphasis on a Russian or Jewish cultural orientation, their financial well-being, stability and relations with American Jewish groups (Ilyin and Kagan 1991; Gorbis 1992; Markowitz 1993; Orleck 1987; Freedman 1993). All three types of organizations—political, religious and entrepreneurial—are found among Soviet Jews in California.

Political Groups

Soviet Jewish political activists were some of the most ideological, ambitious and culturally assertive members of the emigre community. Well established and highly educated, they expressed more moralistic and idealistic concerns than other emigres. Taking their status as refugees seriously, activists hoped to become full participants in American democracy and to remind other Soviet Jews of this mission as well. Demonstrating her outlook, a Bay Area activist described the seriousness with which she approaches American life: "Adjustment is difficult in a different country. It wasn't difficult to find a car or buy an apartment. But language and understanding and reading the papers and realizing at least what's going on and how this country is built and everything, I think for me to live here my whole life doesn't give me enough experience."

Activist emigres are frustrated by what they see as their community's unwillingness to develop well informed positions on significant issues. An engineer described his efforts to foster tolerance in his community: "I find very unattractive feelings among Russian Jews towards Blacks, towards Chinese or other Asians. I had many distressing conversations where I broke relations with many people over this fact. The same is true regarding American communists. I hate American communists, but I wouldn't like them to be outlawed. And this is very hard because not many people feel as strong against communists as I do. But I don't want any group of people to be outlawed because I am trying to see what is good in this society and this should be preserved by any means." Taking a similar position, Herman criticized the authoritarian and conformistic elements of the Russian Jewish personality, which he derided as the "Soviet sickness." "Their general complaint is 'Americans have too much freedom.' How many hours I have spent trying to convince them that you take away this freedom and logically, you will end up with what you are running from." And

Helena suggested that emigres encounter difficulties in adjusting to the States because they put too little thought into their reasons for emigration. "It was like a big number of sheep. Everyone goes, so they should go too. Why? First of all, you have to ask yourself why. And I hate this part of our Russian experience. They are not thinking why they left Russia. They just borrow ideas from other people and follow like sheep."

Activists often function as intermediaries between the Soviet enclave and the larger American Jewish community. Several have been involved in voluntary efforts to resettle just-arrived emigres and held various positions in Jewish-American community bodies. The most ambitious effort undertaken by Los Angeles activists in the mid-1980's sought to unite several interest groups within the emigre population—veterans, doctors and dentists, the elderly, religious and secular constituencies, and the ethnic media—in an umbrella organization called The Association of Soviet Jewish Emigres (ASJE). This organization was founded, after several years of unproductive involvement with the Jewish Federation of Los Angeles (the body that raises money and provides services to the greater Jewish community), by a social service worker, Felix Ryback, along with several other influential emigres. Although they were initially rejected, in 1988, ASJE was awarded a grant by the City of West Hollywood for funds to resettle and serve Soviet Jews.

The success of this organization can be attributed to the frustration felt by those who considered the American Jewish community unresponsive to their needs. An officer of an emigre organization described his feeling of exclusion from the Jewish Federation: "Here we are, already considering ourselves like Americans. Not just immigrants, but already Americans with good experience. A position of irony is that we are still treated as boys and girls. We are not even close to policy making in this country." Such feelings of alienation prompted this activist to develop an organized emigre voice: "So what's going on right now, it's a process of recognition of the Soviet Jews as a power. And I'm doing a lot of things in this matter just to help establish ourself as a real strength."

Precisely because of emigres' close ties to American Jews (the majority of whom share Russian/East European origins and have been crusading for the Soviets' right to emigrate since the 1960s), Soviet Jews have been given little opportunity to assert their own political, cultural, and religious identities in the U.S. Many conflicts between Soviet emigres and their well-meaning American Jewish hosts concerned the Soviet Jews' resettlement. Issues of contention included religious socialization, job placement, community representation, and provision of psychological therapy.

Despite the fact that many immigrant Jews share the concerns of activist emigres, these activists continue to face a great deal of difficulty in organizing the Soviet Jewish enclave. In both San Francisco and Los Angeles, early attempts to create Soviet Jewish community organizations failed. In some cases emigre groups have "different agendas", and this interferes with attempts to organize large groups of people. In Southern California alone, there were three Russian veterans' associations. One merged with American veterans, a second remained independent, and a third focused on the problems of the disabled. Other activists found the lack of consistency in ethnic identification to be a problem. Religious Soviet Jews and those who identified themselves primarily as Russians did not want to participate in the same groups.

And despite the general trend towards conservatism, ideological conflicts sometimes alienated would-be members. For example, two of the most powerful figures in Los Angeles' Soviet Jewish media—the publisher of the community's major newspaper and the producer of a weekly Russian-language television program, (their offices were located in the same building)—refused to cooperate in an organization because of their divergent political views. While the publisher was extremely conservative, the producer was much more moderate.

Even when the emigres were united, activists often found themselves trapped between antagonistic and ill-informed groups representing emigres, on one hand, and the American community, on the other. So before they could teach fellow emigres about the complex web of Jewish organizations and agencies that make policy and offer services, they had to help them understand American Jewish culture. At the same time they needed to educate American Jews about the outlooks held by Soviet immigrants. "Obstacles all over, personal ambition and tension and jealousy. My mentality is that we should not waste time for fights or arguments, we should work harder to get recognition. We have thousands of experienced people. The goal is to continue to make a unit of our community to involve more and more people. To give them a chance to express their talents and serve other people. Because nobody knows better than we our needs."

Soviet Jewish activists' desire to separate themselves from the American Jewish community—while a frequent topic of discussion among emigres—was more an expression of frustration than a serious goal. Rather, they wanted American Jews to take their concerns and perspectives on resettlement policy seriously. In her report on Soviet emigre organizations, Madeleine Tress writes "Sometimes these 'new voices' seem to be in conflict with [American Jewish] federation agencies. It is far more likely that . . . these groups are not in conflict with the North American Jewish communal infrastructure but are beginning the first steps of engagement with it" (Tress 1992: 4).

Emigre activists have hoped to work with their sponsors, but only when the Americans showed more respect. "Our number one goal is to build a strong bridge between the Russian island and the American society and the Jewish community. It is a bridge that should be strong enough to let a thousand people come through. We like our people to be integrated, to be recognized as Jews—don't lose our identity which we barely have. We'd like our kids and our grandchildren to come to the Russian culture."

The Russian Synagogue

Russian language synagogues fill the special religious needs of emigres. As noted in Chapter 4, Soviet Jews' participation in religious activities in the United States is limited, mainly because they were encouraged to assimilate into atheistic Soviet society and had little access to Jewish education or involvement. It is difficult to estimate exactly how many emigres belong to the Chabad-Russian program because attendance fluctuates widely according to the religious occasion being celebrated. Peak attendance was 4,000 persons—more than ten percent of Los Angeles' entire emigre population—for high holiday services in 1993 (Estulin 1993).

Even emigres who are religiously inclined have difficulty in participating in American Jewish life. Much of what Soviet Jews know of the Jewish religion has been passed down from the pre-revolution era and is quite different from the modern, "socially relevant" religion practiced by American Jews today (Gold 1992; Markowitz 1993). Many American synagogues embody a liberal political outlook that the generally conservative Soviet Jews dislike. The most religiously inclined members of the Soviet Jewish population are elderly and know little English or Hebrew—the languages spoken in American synagogues (Freedman 1993).

In Los Angeles, the religious needs of Soviet Jews—especially of elderly men who speak little English—are met by Russian outreach activities of the Chabad-Lubovitch movement. I contacted two of these congregations in Los Angeles. Located in storefronts, each was led by a Russian-speaking rabbi who is himself an immigrant. These rabbis were born into and educated by a tight network of endogamously married rabbinical families that make up the underground Jewish movement of the former Soviet Union. Underground Hassidim in the USSR maintained secret religious services and schools in apartments rather than in the few state-sanctioned synagogues of the Soviet Union (Panish 1981).

These Russian-speaking rabbis are part of a centralized and well organized international Jewish movement that supports their synagogues. One of the rabbis described his organization's appeal to Jewish emigres: "They feel much better, more comfortable with their own community, with their own tradition, with their own language. They come to me after being to American services and they say 'Which kind of synagogue is this?' We give them real *Yiddishkeit*, real Judaism."

The Chabad rabbis utilize humor and enthusiasm to make their activities attractive and enjoyable to Soviet emigres. Services for men are followed by Russian-style meals of bread, salad, herring and free-flowing vodka and whisky. Lively songs and religious lectures, all in Russian, provide a social life for the elderly participants of these congregations. Programming for children is in English and features meals, youthful counselors, group singing, and sports activities.

The Chabad Russian rabbis have been successful in recruiting emigres and expanding their programs. In Los Angeles, Chabad was the most common form of synagogue membership among emigres (Krautman 1990; Gorbis 1992; Tress and Bernick 1992). Nearly all Soviet Jews in Los Angeles—from teenagers to retirees—can name the Chabad-Russian rabbis, while far fewer are familiar with American rabbis or synagogues. In the mid-1980s, the senior Chabad rabbi told me of an ambitious plan to build "a big religious cultural center for the Russian community. Like the West Side Jewish Community Center, with a big synagogue, a big hall to make weddings, bar mitzvahs, everything. With a swimming pool, a health club, with movies and a library. And when we get it, this will unite the community."

At that time, observers both within and outside of the emigre community felt the plan was mere fancy. Yet such a center—built in a remodeled garage—was opened and running in 1994. Inside the lobby, an engraved marble wall honors major contributors including emigre doctors and entrepreneurs as well as recording industry baron David Geffen. During 1994, the Chabad Russian Center offered a variety of activities including High Holiday services for 4,000 and a day camp for 300 youngsters that I mentioned in the introduction. At present, the organization is working with the West Hollywood community to identify a location where they can break ground for their swimming pool (Estulin 1993). According to a leading voice in the emigre community: "Chabad has become the 'in place' for the young elite of the emigre community, such as doctors, dentists, accountants, engineers businessmen, and lawyers. Its Yom Kippur services were attended by over 4,000 emigres. The Russian Community Synagogue has become a major power

center of communal living for Soviet Jews in Los Angeles"
(Gorbis 1992:19).

Entrepreneurs' Groups

Soviet Jewish businesspersons often mobilize their col-
leagues for mutual benefit—sharing information and capital
and finding partners (Orleck 1987). In this way, their joint desire to make a living helps them overcome the individualistic
orientation so widespread in their community. While usually
informal, these networks were well known and easily acces-
sible. Since a quarter of all emigres (and a third of all Soviet
Jewish men) in Los Angeles were self employed, they were
far reaching and inclusive.

Members of entrepreneurial networks tend to have diverse backgrounds; some were professionals in the USSR,
others held clerical jobs. A large proportion had origins in
the Ukrainian Republic, a region noted for its anti-Semitism.
Many claimed that they had developed entrepreneurial and
hustling skills as a means for surviving in a hostile environment. For many members of the business persons' groups,
participation in this informal network offers a non-religious
way for emigres to experience their ethnicity. Mixing business and pleasure, Soviet Jewish entrepreneurs often socialize together. In so doing, they develop the trusting relations
required for cooperative ventures.

The producer of a Los Angeles Russian radio program
described how he relied on ethnic networks and connections
to build his enterprise: "I organized KMNB radio station
and translation service. It stands for "multinational broad-
casting." I opened the service almost 6 years ago for old
people who did not understand English. We translated
American television programs. We got money from people
who would be our future clients—Russian store owners and
even people who wanted to use the service. Then my show
grew, we got bigger shares of money from advertisers because we had the Russian audience. Now I have a cable TV
show. We have Armenian, Polish, Russian and American
viewers. And a lot of businesses like to have advertisements
on the show. They get good publicity and I make money."

In Los Angeles, the business persons' networks grew out of two taxi cooperatives (Russell 1985). In these union-like associations, made up of persons who owned taxi-operators' licenses, emigres set up rules governing taxi drivers' behavior and fought against unlicensed "Gypsy cab" competitors. At the same time, they also developed the allegiances, skills and capital sources that allowed their eventual movement into more extensive self employment activities (Lubin 1985; Halter in Press). The Moscow-born vice president of one cooperative told me how his experience in the group steered him into an ethnic-based entrepreneurial career: "When I got here first, I got a job in a garment factory. I sure wasn't satisfied. And then I found out about this cab association. It's got 201 members, 94 are Russians. And I found out I can make a little more money driving a cab. I worked as a lease driver at first, and in 1978, I bought my own cab. Now I lease it at nights to other Russian drivers." He went on to describe his ideas for the future: "Like most of the others, I'm not going to drive my cab for all my life. I'm planning to go to some kind of different business—a shop or restaurant."

Although ethnic business networks are vital sources of support and capital for emigre entrepreneurs, like most Soviet Jewish organizations, they are periodically fractured by conflicts among their members. Several emigres described being swindled by other refugees and alluded to the personality clashes that arose between co-ethnics. The taxi cooperative vice president described how the previous holder of his position was discharged because he had accepted bribes. "Now we have some people who are against me. We never sing the same song." Despite such reservations, the business persons' networks continued to provide benefits for their members. In the words of an entrepreneur: "It's not necessary to be friends, but we can work together."

A final form of emigre organizational life involves occupational and professional groups. In Los Angeles, over one hundred Soviet Jewish doctors and dentists have established their own organization for professional training and social activities. These doctors' offices are often adjacent to neighborhoods where Russian emigres live. Russian emigres prefer to visit Russian-speaking physicians, and Soviet Jewish doctors willingly accept fellow refugees' government-provided health benefits. Soviet emigres have also created associations involving engineers, scientists and artists in California and throughout the U.S. (Gorbis 1992; Illyn and Kagan 1991; Markowitz 1993).

RELATIONS WITH JEWISH AGENCIES

American Jews have devoted extensive effort and good will to the resettlement of Soviet Jewry. Soviet Jews are grateful, but the problems of religious, cultural and linguistic incompatibility, as described in the last chapter, sometime provokes emigres' resentment towards their American sponsors, causing some to limit contacts with American Jews (Gitelman 1985). An initial source of conflict with American Jews arises in the context of resettlement interactions—both in terms of service delivery and cultural socialization (Gitelman 1978; Gold 1987; 1992). Emigres often complained that they were not assisted in ways that they desired (Dorf and Katlin 1983).

The difficulties involved in resettlement result from the near impossibility of the task at hand. No matter how well-funded a resettlement agency or how skillful its staff, the major goals of resettlement—economic self-sufficiency and cultural adjustment—are difficult to attain. Economic self-sufficiency is largely dependent upon economic factors beyond any resettlement worker's control. Similarly, cultural adjustment, learning English, and resolving the mental trauma brought on by the refugee experience can only be achieved through the efforts of refugees themselves, expended over protracted periods of time.

Further complicating matters, resettlement interactions frequently take place in an environment of extensive cultural incompatibility between providers and recipients of services. To do their job at all, resettlement agencies, schools and the like must engage in a great deal of client socialization. For many refugees, resettlement staff are the first representatives of American society with whom they have any significant contact. As a consequence, even the most basic interactions between refugees and resettlement staff involve various forms of cultural conflict. In the words of one government report on refugee resettlement: "there are aspects of the American life with which refugees must simply learn to cope." (Cichon et al. 1986: 87).

Training Refugees to Receive Therapy

In Chapter 3, I discussed emigres' conflicts with resettlement agencies over job placement. Another area where misunderstandings arise is in the provision of psychological therapy. Health assessments have shown that refugees suffer from a variety of mental health problems (Brod and Huertin-Roberts 1992). Consequently, the government and resettlement agencies have established mental health programs for this population. Unfortunately, Soviet Jews often lack the cultural prerequisites for a successful, American-style therapy interaction: they are generally unwilling to confide in bureaucrats and remain skeptical about the subconscious motivation of behavioral problems.

Social workers and therapists who work with Soviet refugees describe extensive cultural conflicts based on mistrust, the stigmatized status of mental health problems in the USSR, and the fact that mental illness was generally handled with medication rather than psychological therapy. "Depression, for example, is perceived in the Soviet Union as a biological entity and bio-chemical treatment is offered. A refugee client experiencing depression, therefore, expects to be treated with a pill. A service provider who attempts to deal with the depression through a commonly used method of talking therapy is not only perceived as strange but is also viewed as incompetent as the client doesn't receive what he/she thinks is needed." (Drachman and Halberstadt 1992:73).

Finally, most refugees do not see a connection between the process of therapy and the problems that, for them, are most pressing. "I like you." said one Soviet client to her social worker. "You're a nice lady and this way I can practice my English. But I don't really understand how talking about this will help me." (Dorf and Katlin 1983: 152).

Religious Socialization

Another area of conflict involves the religious socialization element of resettlement. Emigres often resent the condescending way that they were approached by agency staff (De Voe 1981; Indra 1987). In retrospect, it is easy to see how the attitude expressed in *The Journal of Jewish Communal Service* could alienate Soviet Jews, who after all, are refugees from an autocratic society: "Rabbi Posner says we have to 'create a Jewish need in him' just as we would with a child, while at the same time understanding that he is no child" (Goldberg 1981: 161). "It is absolutely essential to exploit ESL (English as a second language) classes . . . where they are actually a captive audience. . . for inculcating Jewish attitudes and values" (Schiff 1980: 45-49). Emigres bristle at American Jews' assertion that they should have settled in Israel or that because they lack religious knowledge, they are not "real Jews."

Conflicts involving religious and cultural socialization were most marked during the early years of resettlement (prior to the mid-1980s) when media exposure to the image of the pious refusenik led American Jews assume that Soviet Jews would be both religious and anti-Soviet (Barber 1987). Markowitz describes American Jews' rejection of the newcomers upon discovering that the idealized Sharansky [a leading Soviet Jewish dissident who became a cause celebre during his long imprisonment] image did not always apply: "As American Jews found some of the ways that Soviet Jews act to be alien, they came to label these behaviors and the individuals associated with them not 'Jewish' but 'Russian'" (Markowitz 1988a: 84).

By the late 1980s, official acknowledgment was finally given to the fact that most Soviet Jews were not religiously active. Initial hopes to "create a Jewish need" were replaced by more a realistic acknowledgment of Soviet emigres' secular and ethnic (rather than religious) identification (Carp 1990). An American rabbi who works with Soviet Jews reflected this new awareness: "One of the disappointments that many rabbis felt was that most of the Soviet Jews did not find a need to express their Jewishness. We should have understood this, because they come from a secular, atheistic country, but it was difficult to accept."(Barber 1987: 41).

Emigres also experienced ideological conflicts with American Jews. Soviet Jews disliked being called "Noshrim" (dropouts) for not settling in Israel (Cullen 1989; Jacobsen 1978). Whenever Jewish agencies discussed measures to force Soviets to settle in the Jewish State, emigres expressed their displeasure, and pointed out the hypocrisy of such statements, saying "let my people go, indeed!" In the words of a Los Angeles activist: "I have to say that I've heard a lot of statements on behalf of American Jews, okay, which I can only describe as a double standard. Why should they sit in Beverly Hills and accuse me of not going over to Israel and I left Russia with $120 and he has all the money in the world? I accept criticism on behalf of those who are in Israel. But I am absolutely reluctant to accept any criticism on behalf of those who live in the United States. If we are accused of making it easy for ourselves [by not moving to Israel], they can be accused of twice as much."

In sum, culture-based conflicts in several areas of service delivery are challenging to resettlement staff and clients alike. Unfortunately, the conflicts I have described characterize much of the interaction between Soviet Jews and American Jewish agencies. When people in the two communities develop images of each other in a hostile setting, it is no wonder that negative views often overwhelm the good will that both parties bring to their relations.

Cultural Differences

When outside of the agency setting, Russian emigres and American Jews have many different attitudes and social habits. Russians generally think Americans are superficial and lacking in passion and warmth. To make this point, Mila contrasted an American wedding with a Russian one. "Big things like weddings, anniversaries, parties are just done in a different way. A Russian wedding, I mean you go all out. You have the whole synagogue. You have the wedding in the chapel and then there's a huge reception. Huge meals and appetizers and an emcee and a band and flowers and balloons and God knows what else. It's like a big occasion. Where Americans, they're like, 'well the wedding's at seven and we'll leave by nine and just have appetizers—cheese and crackers.'" Reflecting their general view of American Jews' social ineptitude, many emigres feel that American Jews are not very supportive or generous to them. Zoya described how she felt rejected by the members of the Southern California synagogue that she attended. "When I moved here, I joined Sinai Temple and I saw people over there didn't like me. I wanted to be involved, but people didn't accept me. I didn't feel myself to be equal and people did not feel me to be equal and that was very painful. So I don't go any more. I think I am as close to God in any other place as in the temple." More than one emigre attributed bad relations with American Jews to their hosts' jealousy. "See our Russian community, we are successful and nobody helps us. They think 'you should work hard but not be successful. To work in McDonalds, this is your place.'"

Soviet Jews' shared dislike of American values and cultural patterns as well as their feelings of rejection by American Jews is a reason many turn away from American Jews. Generally conservative, emigres often complain about gays, minority groups, graffiti, the crime rate, drug use, pornography and lack of discipline in schools. While retaining a fear of anti-Semitism, they nevertheless have a strong identity as whites and sometimes make disparaging comments about Blacks and Asians (Markowitz 1993). As refugees from communism, they are especially incensed by liberals (heavily represented in the American Jewish community) who oppose nuclear power, distrust the military, and demand civil liberties for social misfits.

American Jews tend to be Democrats; most Soviet Jews are politically conservative and when they become naturalized citizens, join the Republican party (Gold 1992; Noonan 1988; Markowitz 1993; Lipset 1992). A recent article describes Jews from the former Soviet Union as "a community that is staunchly conservative Republican and is quite puzzled by the left leaning liberalism of American Jews" (Frumkin 1993: 17). A Soviet Jewish journalist observes that "most American Jews are used to being liberals. But Russian

Jews, having very tough experience, know what socialism does mean. They are very close to the right wing, politically. I think that almost everybody voted for Republicans." As these examples show, the cultural, linguistic and political differences between Soviet emigres and American Jews are enduring, and as such, continue to shape the two groups' patterns of interaction.

CONCLUSIONS

Soviet Jews' patterns of adaptation to the U.S. have followed neither the Jewish assimilation nor ethnic solidarity models in the way experts might have predicted. They have not merged with American Jews nor set up strong, community-wide organizations. Skilled, educated and well served by American Jewish agencies, these new immigrants have fewer reasons for organizing their communities than was the case among the immigrant Jews of an earlier generation who had few resources beyond their own organizations for satisfying basic needs. Most prefer the company of fellow emigres in an informal context that emphasizes their Russian culture and politically conservative views.

The general consensus regarding former Soviet Jews' communal lives suggests that they are not heavily involved in formal organizations. However, that image is beginning to be countered by several embryonic forms of ethnic mobilization. Groups moving towards organization include political activists, Russian-oriented religious congregations, business owners and health professionals. Regardless of their collective orientation, Jews from the former Soviet Union will shape a community and identity that is uniquely their own—in their own way and in their own time.

6

Conclusions

REFLECTIONS ON AMERICAN LIFE

It has now been over 15 years since the first major wave of Soviet Jews entered the U.S. With a decade and a half of American experience behind them, how do these emigres view their lives? Upon arriving in the United States, Jews from the former Soviet Union are often overwhelmed by the vastly different surroundings they confront. This was especially the case for those who left before the end of the Soviet system, because they had little information about American life and their environment was drastically different from that in the capitalist West.

More recent arrivals have much more familiarity with aspects of American life than was the case prior to the 1990s. The mass media and Western consumer culture have become far more available in the former Soviet Union. International travel both to and from the former USSR has increased. More recent emigres frequently have had some exposure to typically Western institutions like party politics, capitalist economics and extensive involvement in religion. At the same time, Western social problems like homelessness, unemployment and gross economic inequality are far more evident than in the former Soviet Union during the communist period. Whether they came before or after 1990, differences in culture, economics, geography, and lifestyle between the Russia and the U.S. remain enormous. Emigres often compare the experience of arriving in the States with landing on Mars: "It's not just a different country, it's a different planet." Many of the emigres' initial reactions are predictable. They are overwhelmed by the opulence of American society. Often, they are disturbed by the excesses of American freedom, especially drugs, sexuality, and anti-authoritarianism. They are horrified by America's violence and depressed by its shallowness, commercialism, and low cultural standards. Reacting to his new environment in the 1980s, a recently arrived doctor asserted that America has "too much freedom and too little order ... I think America must be stronger. I saw so many people at an anti-nuclear demonstration. It's bad. American people don't try to help their government. I think it's too much freedom here, too much. West Germany, it's better. Not so much freedom, but order. They can go out at night on the street."

In coping with their new environment head on, emigres devote themselves to the practical matter of building a new life. In the words of a former engineer who now runs a body shop: "America is a crazy country. But it is still good. Here, we still have a chance." One indication of emigres' feelings about adaptation is the fact that their naturalization rates are the highest of all refugee populations (ORR 1993). Rather than dwelling on the past, many simply concern themselves with the present. Zoya described her outlook on adaptation: "You know, what I think helps me is that I cut it. When my mama and papa sometime say 'At home it was so and so.' I say, 'No, your home is here.' They cannot forget about it. But I made myself forget. No Russia anymore. I never was Russian. I was a Jew and I am a Jew." Especially for those who came to the United States at an early age, Russia is just a distant memory. Misha, a body shop owner, reflected on his life since migrating: "When I first came to this country, I saw a couple of Russian movies and it was so real to me. But yesterday, I saw this Russian movie and it was for me so strange because its five years since I left Russia. It's a long time and those problems and even the humor and everything, its kind of a fog. I just left the movie before the end. I have no feelings about Russia as a matter of fact. My life is in my business and in this country, so I'm just starting to forget all this Russian life. To some extent, its kind of a relief."

SOVIET JEWISH EMIGRES: UNIQUE ASPECTS

The experience of Jews from the former Soviet Union casts light on our understanding of contemporary immigration by reminding us that we cannot glibly generalize about "all immigrants" from the experiences of Asian, Latin American or Caribbean groups.

Unlike most other immigrants who come from nations which have less developed government bureaucracies and offer fewer services than the United States, Jews from the former Soviet Union must unlearn a whole set of expectations and techniques developed in the context of the Soviet bureaucracy. Used to securing what they needed from government, now they must fill their needs through personal initiative. Most emigres make impressive progress in their adjustment to the free market economy. Others, however, become frustrated when they cannot find desired jobs and react by blaming the resettlement system.

Because they come from a country where the government, until recently, controlled all organizational life, Soviet Jews immediately regard any type of organization with a great deal of cynicism. Despite the potential benefits that could be achieved through collective action, would-be community leaders are assumed to be self-serving. And while Soviet Jews are a religiously-defined group with a strong ethnic identity, their lack of experience with voluntary organizations, atheistic orientation, and desire to avoid indoctrination hinder their active participation in the many religious services and programs offered to them by the American Jewish community.

Whereas most recent immigrants to the U.S. must learn to face life here as a minority group, Soviet Jews leave their minority status behind. They are often surprised by the extent to which Jews and other American groups openly display their religious and ethnic membership, and frequently discuss the radical transformation of their ethnic and national identity now that they live in the United States.

Ironically, after decades of striving for acceptance in the Soviet Union, it is only in the U.S. that Soviet Jews have, in a sense, become Russians. Andre explained: "In Russia, our attempts to be Russian was taken by Russians as an offense because they believed we are Jewish. We weren't Jewish because we didn't have Jewish culture and we weren't Russian because we were not accepted as Russians. So we lost wherever we went. We came here, and finally here, they call us Russians—just at the moment when we want to be American. Isn't that funny? What I am is Jewish with Russian culture living in the United States and trying to be American. This is as much as we can do in this situation."

SOVIET JEWS AND THE IMMIGRANT EXPERIENCE

Of course, as immigrants, Soviet Jews also share many experiences with other newcomers to the U.S. Like all immigrants and refugees, Soviet Jews must rebuild their lives, families, and communities in the U.S. They must master a culture and language which, to them, is exotic and strange.

Like other immigrants, Jews from the former Soviet Union must find work in the U.S. Here, their experiences are similar in many ways to those of other skilled and educated groups like Koreans, Asian Indians, and Filipinos. Some find reasonably good jobs in the existing economy, others become self employed. Like other skilled groups, many suffer a loss of social prestige as they try to rebuild a career in a new society. As many achieve economic stability and relative mastery of the English language and American culture, they also continue to prize their own culture and community, and consequently, emphasize Russian contacts and content in their social lives.

SOVIET JEWS AND THE HISTORY OF AMERICAN JEWISH IMMIGRATION

This is not the first time that a large number of Jews have entered the United States from Russia. In fact, consideration of the long-term experience of earlier cohorts can offer valuable lessons for understanding the experience of present day emigres.

Before the turn of the century, the majority of American Jews were of German descent. As a group, they were more Westernized, educated and immersed in Anglo-American culture than the over two million Eastern-European Jews who arrived between 1880 and 1924. In the face of this enormous inflow, German-American Jews planned a program that involved training Russian immigrants to become self-reliant, assimilated Americans as quickly as possible (Farber et al. 1988; Joselit 1983). German Jews sincerely worked to aid the "greenhorns," attempted to consolidate their power over the entire religious community, and feared that the presence of a large mass of unassimilated and often radical co-religionists would provoke anti-Semitism among native Protestants.

Early in the century, German Jews created a number of community organizations, many of which are still in existence. These include the United Hebrew Charities, HIAS (Hebrew Immigrant Aid Society), the Hawthorne School (a Jewish reformatory), and other Jewish communal organizations that provide job placements, English lessons, interest-free loans, health care, and summer camps for recent immigrants. Several now currently serve today's Soviet Jewish immigrants.

Early in the century, the Americanizing project was often harsh and condescending. An American Jewish publication asserted that new immigrants "must be Americanized in spite of themselves, in the mode prescribed by their friends and benefactors" (Howe 1976:235). A major goal of the Americanizers was to "pull down the [Jewish] ghetto" in the Lower East Side (of Manhattan) and distribute the recently arrived brethren around the nation, thus restricting their ability to reestablish enclaves where old-world outlooks and practices would be preserved. Despite the Americanizing program's arrogant attitude, many mobility-seeking offspring of Russian Jews complied with its activities. Others resisted and instead created organizations intended to preserve Eastern European Jewish beliefs, tradition, politics, culture and language (Gorelick 1981; Rischin 1962).

As a result, Russian Jewish newcomers feuded with the German-American establishment to the point of creating parallel community institutions, such as hospitals and communal organizations, that reflected the new group's culture and place of settlement. In New York, the established Germans became known as "uptown Jews" in contrast to the more humble, immigrant Russian "downtown Jews" of the Lower East Side. With time, however, relations between German and Russian Jews smoothed and a "wiser policy of gradual adjustment" was agreed upon—one in which immigrants themselves came to play a leading role (Howe 1976: 236). Faced with the common threats of anti-Semitism and the Holocaust, and inspired by Israel, the two groups eventually became united in numerous political, economic, and philanthropic endeavors (Goren 1970; Farber et al. 1988; Gold and Phillips in press).

Following this precedent, we can assume that as time passes, Soviet Jews will cease being the dependent subjects of the American Jewish community, which in turn, will become more accepting and less dictatorial in their relations with the newcomers. Instead, like the Russian Jews who were resettled by their German-American co-ethnics early in this century, the former Soviets will become yet another subgroup of the diverse Jewish-American population. Their presence will color the Jewish-American community and, eventually, they will sit at the table alongside their one-time hosts (Rischin 1962; Gorelick 1981; Wirth 1928).

As today's emigres often point out, recently arrived Jews from the former USSR are drastically different from the cohort of their *landsleit* (countrymen) who came to these shores from Russia almost a century ago. They want to be accepted on their own terms. They care deeply about the traditions of their European way of life and, while grateful to America for the opportunities and freedom it offers, they strongly guard their independence from established Jews and others who they see as over-zealously planning their acculturation. What remains to be seen is the extent to which these emigres will become involved in organized communal life in the future— either on their own or in consort with American Jews.

References

Abrams, Israel
  1911 "Jews" in Encyclopedia Britannica, Eleventh Edition, Vol. XV.
        Pp. 371-410.

Adorno, T.W., Else Frenkel-Brunswik, Daniel J. Levinson and R. Nevitt
Sanford
  1950 The Authoritarian Personality. New York: Harper Brothers.

Andreski, Stanislav
  1979 "Communism and the Jews in Eastern Europe." International
        Journal of Comparative Sociology 20 (1-2):151-161.

Aronowitz, Michael
  1984 "The Social and Emotional Adjustment of Immigrant Children:
        A Review of the Literature" International Migration Review
        (18)2: 237-257.

Baca-Zinn, Maxine and D. Stanley Eitzen
  1987 Diversity in American Families. New York: Harper and Row.

Bailey, Thomas and Roger Waldinger
  1991 "Primary, Secondary and Enclave Labor Markets: A Training
        Systems Approach." American Sociological Review 56: 432-45.

Barber, Jennifer
  1987 "The Soviet Jews of Washington Heights" New York Affairs 10
        (1):34-43

Bellah, Robert, Richard Madsen, William M. Sullivan, Ann Swidler, and
Steven M. Tipton
  1985 Habits of the Heart: Individualism and Commitment in Ameri-
        can Life. Berkeley: University of California Press.

Bonacich, Edna
  1973 "A Theory of Middleman Minorities." American Sociological
        Review 37 (October):547-559.

Breton, Raymond
  1964 "Institutional Completeness of Ethnic Communities and the
        Personal Relations of Immigrants." American Journal of Sociol-
        ogy 84: 293-318.

Brod, Meryl and Suzanne Heurtin-Roberts
  1992   "Older Russian Emigres and Medical Care" Western Journal of Medicine 157 (3):333-336

Brym, Robert J.
  1985   "The Changing Rate of Jewish Emigration from the USSR: Some Lessons from the 1970s" Soviet Jewish Affairs 15(2): 23-44.

  1993   "The Emigration Potential of Jews in the Former Soviet Union" East European Jewish Affairs 23(2): 9-24.

Calhoun, Craig (ed.)
  1994   Social Theory and the Politics of Identity. Oxford UK: Blackwell

Carp, Joel M.
  1990   "Absorbing Jews Jewishly: Professional Responsibility for Jewishly Absorbing New Immigrants in their New Communities" Journal of Jewish Communal Service 66(4): 366-374.

  1992   "Leadership Development in the Emigre Community" pp. 35-39 in Madeleine Tress and Deborah Bernick (editors) New Voices: The Integration of Soviet Emigres and Their Organizations Into the Jewish Communal World. New York: Council of Jewish Federations.

Chesler, Evan
  1974   The Russian Jewry Reader. New York: Behrman House Inc.

Chiswick, Barry
  1993   "Soviet Jews in the United States: An Analysis of Their Linguistic and Economic Adjustment" International Migration Review 27 (102):260-285

  1995   "Soviet Jews in the United States: Language and Labor Market Adjustments Revisited" Mimeo, Department of Economics, University of Illinois at Chicago.

Cichon, Donald J., Elizabeta M. Gozdziak and Jane G. Grover
  1986   The Economic and Social Adjustment of Non-Southeast Asian Refugees, Volume I: Analysis Across Cases. Dover, New Hampshire: Research Management Corporation.

CJF (Council of Jewish Federations)
  1993   Immigration Data (mimeo)

Collins, Beth, Melissa Glazer, Cara Kates, Jilla Lavian, Ellen Rabin, Dan Rathblatt, Robin Segal
  1986   Family and Community Among Iranian Jews in Los Angeles. Masters Thesis, Hebrew Union College and University of Southern California

Coughlin, Maria and Regina Rosenberg
  1983   "Health Education and Beyond: A Soviet Women's Group Experience" Journal of Jewish Communal Service 60(1):65-69.

Cummings, Scott, ed.
1980 Self-Help in Urban America: Patterns of Minority Business En-
      terprise. Port Washington, N.Y.: Kennikat Press.

Cunningham, Marina and Nina Dorf
1979 "Prenatal Group for Soviet Immigrants." Journal of Jewish
      Communal Service LVI (1): 73-76

Davis, Mike
1990 City of Quartz. London: Verso

de Voe, Dorsh
1981 "Framing Refugees as Clients" International Migration Review
      15(1):88-94.

Di Franceisco, Wayne and Zvi Gitelman
1984 "Soviet Political Culture and Covert Participation in Policy Im-
      plementation" American Political Science Review 78 (3): 603-
      621.

Dinnerstein, Leonard, Roger L. Nichols and David M. Reimers
1990 Natives and Strangers: Blacks, Indians and Immigrants in
      America, Second Edition. New York: Oxford University Press.

Di Paz, Michel
1994 "Zhirinovsky's Follies" Jewish Journal (Los Angeles) April 22-
      28: 17.

Dorf, Nina and Fay Katlin
1983 "The Soviet Jewish Immigrant Client: Beyond Resettlement."
      Journal of Jewish Communal Service 60 (2): 146-154.

Drachman, Diane and Anna Halberstadt
1992 "A Stage of Migration Framework As Applied to Recent Society
      Emigres" Pp. 63-78 in Angela Shen Ryan (ed.), Social Work with
      Immigrants and Refugees. New York: Haworth Press.

Eckles, Timothy J., Lawrence J. Lewin, David S. North and Dangole J.
Spakevicius
1982 "A Portrait in Diversity: Voluntary Agencies and The Office of
      Refugee Resettlement Matching Grant Program." Lewin and
      Associates.

Estulin, Naftoli
1993 "Chabad Russian Immigrant Program and Synagogue." Leaf-
      let, September.

Farber, Bernard, Charles H. Mindel and Bernard Lazerwitz
1988 "The Jewish American Family." Pp. 400-437 in Charles H. Min-
      del, Robert Habenstein and Roosevelt Wright, Jr. (editors) Eth-
      nic Families in America, third edition. New York: Elsevier

Federation of Jewish Philanthropies of New York
1985 Jewish Identification and Affiliation of Soviet Jewish Immi-
      grants in New York City -- A Needs Assessment and Planning
      Study.

Frankel-Paul, Ellen and Jacobs, Dan N.
  1981 "The New Soviet Migration in Cincinnati" in Jacobs and Frankel-Paul (eds.) Studies in the Third Wave: Recent Migrations of Soviet Jews to the U.S. Boulder: The Westview Press. pp. 77-114.

Franklin, John Hope
  1992 "Ethnicity in American Life: The Historical Perspective" Pp. 14-20 in Virginia Cyrus (ed) Experiencing Race, Class and Gender in the United States. Mountain View, CA: Mayfield.

Freedman, Robert O. (ed.)
  1984 Soviet Jewry in the Decisive Decade, 1971-80. Durham, North Carolina: Duke Press.

  _____

  1989 Soviet Jewry in the 1980s: The Politics of Anti-Semitism and Emigration and the Dynamics of Resettlement. Durham, North Carolina: Duke Press.

Freedman, Jenny A.
  1993 "Soviet Jews, Orthodox Judaism, and the Lubavitcher Hasidim" East European Jewish Affairs 1 (23): 57-77.

Fruchtbaum, Irene and Rodney Skager
  1989 "Influence of Parental Values on Dating Behavior of Young Russian Women: A Cross-Cultural Perspective" UCLA Department of Education.

Gans, Herbert
  1979 "Symbolic Ethnicity; The Future of Ethnic Groups and Cultures in America" Ethnic and Racial Studies 2(1): 1-20.

GAO (US General Accounting Office)
  1990 Soviet Refugees: Processing and Admittance to the United States. GAO/NSIAD-90-158.

Gilison, Jerome M.
  1981 "The Resettlement of Soviet Jewish Emigres: Results of a Survey in Baltimore." Pp. 29-56 in Studies in the Third Wave: Recent Migrations of Soviet Jews to the U.S., edited by Dan N. Jacobs and Ellen Frankel-Paul. Boulder, Colorado: Westview Press.

Gitelman, Zvi
  1978 "Soviet Immigrants and American Absorption Efforts: A Case Study in Detroit." Journal of Jewish Communal Service 55 (1) 77-82.

  _____

  1981 "Soviet Jewish Immigrants to the United States: Profile, Problems, Prospects" Paper delivered at the Baltimore Hebrew College, May 3.

  _____

  1985 "The Quality of Life in Israel and the United States" Pp. 47-68 in New Lives: The Adjustment of Soviet Jewish Immigrants in the

United States and Israel, edited by Rita J. Simon. Lexington, Massachusetts: Lexington Books.

Gitlin, Todd
1994 "From Universalism to Difference: Notes on the Fragmentation of the Idea of the Left" pp. 150-174 in Calhoun, Craig (ed.) Social Theory and the Politics of Identity. Oxford UK: Blackwell.

Glazer, Nathan and Daniel Patrick Moynihan
1963 Beyond the Melting Pot. Cambridge: The MIT Press.

Goffman, Erving
1961 Asylums: Essays on the Social Situation of Mental Patients and Other Inmates. Garden City New York: Anchor.

Gold, Steven J.
1985 "Refugee Communities: Soviet Jewish and Vietnamese Refugees in the San Francisco Bay Area." Doctoral Dissertation, University of California, Berkeley.

_____
1986 "Style of Activism Among Refugee Communities: The Case of Soviet Jews and Vietnamese." Kroeber Anthropology Papers, No. 65-66: 35-48.

_____
1987 "Dealing with Frustration: A Study of Interactions Between Resettlement Staff and Refugees." Pp. 108-128 in People in Upheaval, edited by Scott Morgan and Elizabeth Colson. New York: Center For Migration Studies.

_____
1988a "Refugees and Small Business: The Case of Soviet Jews and Vietnamese" Ethnic and Racial Studies, Vol. 11 (4): 411-438.

_____
1988b "Patterns of Interaction and Adjustment Among Soviet Jewish Refugees" Contemporary Jewry 9 (2):87-105

_____
1989 "Differential Adjustment Among New Immigrant Family Members." Journal of Contemporary Ethnography 17 (4): 408-434.

_____.
1991 "Nascent Mobilization in a New Immigrant Community: The Case of Soviet Jews in California." Research in Community Sociology, Volume 2: 185-208.

_____
1992 Refugee Communities: A Comparative Field Study. Newbury Park, CA: Sage.

_____
1994 Soviet Jews in the United States. American Jewish Yearbook 94 1994: 3-57.

Gold, Steven and Bruce Phillips
in press "Mobility and Continuity among Eastern European Jews" in
Sylvia Pedraza and Ruben G. Rumbaut (eds.) Origins and Des-
tinies: Immigration, Race and Ethnicity in America. Belmont,
CA: Wadsworth.

Gold, Steven and Mia Tuan
1993 "Jews from the former Soviet Union in the United States" New
Faces of Liberty.

Goldberg, Simcha R.
1981 "Jewish Acculturation and the Soviet Immigrant." Journal of
Jewish Communal Service 57 (3):154-163.

Goldscheider, Calvin and Frances E. Kobrin.
1980 "Ethnic Continuity and the Process of Self-Employment." Ethnicity 7: 256-278

Goldscheider, Calvin and Alan S. Zuckerman.
1984 The Transformation of The Jews. Chicago: University of Chicago Press

Goodman, Jerry
1984 "The Jews in the Soviet Union: Emigration and its Difficulties"
pp. 17-28 in Robert O. Freedman (ed.) Soviet Jewry in the Decisive Decade

1971-1980. Durham: Duke University Press.

Gorbis, Boris Z.
1992 "Give Us Your Poor Homeless Organizations: A Review of California's Soviet-Jewish Organizations" pp. 17-23 in Madeleine
Tress and Deborah Bernick (editors) New Voices: The Integration of Soviet Emigres and Their Organizations Into the Jewish
Communal World. New York: Council of Jewish Federations.

Gordon, Milton
1964 Assimilation in American Life. New York: Oxford.

Gorelick, Sherry
1981 City College and the Jewish Poor. New York: Schocken Books.

Goren, Arthur A.
1970 New York Jews and the Quest for Community. New York: Columbia University Press.

Greenbaum, Leonora
1985 "Two Families, Three Generation: One Story." Pp. 69-89 in New
Lives: The Adjustment of Soviet Jewish Immigrants in the United States and Israel, edited by Rita J. Simon. Lexington, Massachusetts: Lexington Books.

Halter, Marilyn
Forthcoming "Ethnicity and the Entrepreneur: Self-Employment among
Former Soviet Jewish Refugees" in Marilyn Halter (ed.) Ethnicity and Urban Enterprise: New Migrants to Massachusetts. University of Massachusetts Press.

HIAS (Hebrew Immigrant Aid Society)
1991   Annual Statistics 1979-1991. New York: HIAS

1993   Annual Statistics New York: HIAS

1995   Annual Statistics New York: HIAS

Horowitz, Bethamie
1993   The 1991 New York Jewish Population Study. New York: United Jewish Appeal -- Federation of Jewish Philanthropies of New York

Howe, Irving
1976   World of Our Fathers. New York: Bantam Books.

Hulewat, Phillis
1981   "Dynamics of the Soviet Jewish Family: Its Impact on Clinical Practice for the Jewish Family Agency." Journal of Jewish Communal Service LVIII (1):53-60.

Hyfler, Robert
1991   "When is a Refugee No Longer a Refugee and Other Post-Resettlement Observations" Journal of Jewish Communal Service, (Spring): 285-88.

Ingram, Judith
1994   "Zhirinovsky's Blames Jews" Lansing State Journal, (November 10): 8A.

Ilyin, Pavel and Mikaella Kagan
1991   "Finding a Niche in American Jewish Institutional Life – Soviet Jewish Emigre Organizations" Paper presented at the Wilstein Institute for Jewish Policy Studies Conference, Soviet Jewish Acculturation – Beyond Resettlement, Palo Alto

Ivry, Joann
1992   "Paraprofessionals in Refugee Resettlement" Pp. 99-117 in Angela Shen Ryan (ed.), Social Work with Immigrants and Refugees. New York: Haworth Press.

Jacobs, Dan N.
1981   "Introduction." in Jacobs and Frankel Paul (eds.) Studies of the Third Wave: Recent Migrations of Soviet Jews to the United States. Boulder Colorado: Westview Press. pp. 1-10.

Jacobs, Dan N. and Ellen Frankel Paul(eds.)
1981   Studies of the Third Wave: Recent Migrations of Soviet Jews to the United States. Boulder Colorado: Westview Press.

Jacobson, Gaynor I.
1978   "Soviet Jewry: Perspectives on the 'Dropout' Issue. Journal of Jewish Communal Service LV (1): 83-89

Jewish Family Service of the North Shore
1990 Social Need Survey of Immigrants to the North Shore from the Soviet Union.

Joselit, Jenna Weissman.
1983 Our Gang: Jewish Crime and the New York Jewish Community, 1900-1940. Bloomington: Indiana University Press.

Kahan, Arcadius
1986 Essays in Jewish Social and Economic History. Chicago: University of Chicago Press.

Karklins, Rasma
1987 "Determinants of Ethnic Identification in the USSR: The Soviet Jewish Case." Ethnic and Racial Studies 10(1):27-47.

Kestin, Hesh
1985 "Making Cheese from Snow" Forbes (July 29): 90-95

Kim, Illsoo
1981 New Urban Immigrants: The Korean Community in New York. Princeton, N.J.: Princeton University Press.

Kliger, Hannah
1989 "Ethnic Voluntary Associations in Israel" The Jewish Journal of Sociology 31(2): 109-118.

Kochan, Lionel (ed.)
1978 The Jews in Soviet Russia Since 1917. London: Oxford University Press

Kosmin, Barry
1990 The Class of 1979: The 'Acculturation' of Jewish Immigrants from the Soviet Union. New York: Council of Jewish Federations

_____
1991 Exploring and Understanding the Findings of the 1990 National Jewish Population Survey. Paper Prepared for Hollander Colloquium. Los Angeles (July)

Kosmin, Barry and Jeffrey Scheckner
1994 Jewish Population in the United States. American Jewish Yearbook Vol. 94

Kozulin, Alex and Alex Venger
1993 "Psychological and Learning Problems of Immigrant Children from the Former Soviet Union" Journal of Jewish Communal Service (Fall):64-72.

Krautman, Jerry Allan
1990 A Study of The Acculturation and Jewish Identity of Soviet Jews Emigrating to Los Angeles Between 1972 and 1989. MBA Thesis, University of Judaism.

Kuznets, Simon
1975 "Immigration of Russian Jews to the United States: Background and Structure" Perspectives in American History 9: 35-124.

Levkova, Ilya I.
1984 "Adaptation and Acculturation of Soviet Jews in the United States: A Preliminary Analysis" pp. 109-143 in Robert O. Freedman (ed.) Soviet Jewry in the Decisive Decade 1971-1980. Durham: Duke University Press.

Lieberson, Stanley
1981 A Piece of the Pie. Berkeley: University of California Press.

Light, Ivan
1972 Ethnic Enterprise in America: Business and Welfare among Chinese, Japanese and Blacks. Berkeley: University of California Press.

1979 "Disadvantaged Minorities in Self-Employment." International Journal of Comparative Sociology XX (1-2):31-45.

1980 "Asian Entrepreneurs in America" pp. 33-57 in Scott Cummings (ed.) Self Help in Urban America: Patterns of Minority Business Enterprise. Port Washington, NY: Kennikat Press

1984 "Immigrant and Ethnic Enterprise in North America." Ethnic and Racial Studies 17 (2):195-216.

1985 "Immigrant Entrepreneurs in America: Koreans in Los Angeles" in Nathan Glazer (ed.) Clamor at the Gates: The New American Immigration. San Francisco: Institute for Contemporary Studies. pp 161-178.

Light, Ivan and Edna Bonacich
1988 Immigrant Entrepreneurs. Berkeley: University of California Press.

Light, Ivan, Mehdi Bozorgmehr and Claudia Der-Martirosian
1991 "The Four Iranian Ethnic Economies in Los Angeles." Paper presented at the Annual Meeting of The American Sociological Association, Cincinnati, Aug 23-27.

Lipset, Seymour Martin.
1990 "A Unique People in an Exceptional Country." Pp. 3-29 in American Pluralism and the Jewish Community, edited by Seymour Martin Lipset. New Brunswick, N.J. Transaction.

Littman, Mark
1993 Office of Refugee Resettlement Monthly Data Report for September 1992. Washington, DC: Office of Refugee Resettlement.

Lubin, Nancy
1985 "Small Business Owners." Pp. 151-164 in New Lives: The Adjustment of Soviet Jewish Immigrants in the United States and Israel, edited by Rita J. Simon. Lexington, Massachusetts: Lexington Books.

Lyman, Stanford
1974 Chinese Americans. New York: Random House.

_____
1977 The Asian in North America. Santa Barbara: ABC Clio.

Mangiafico, Luciano
1988 Contemporary American Immigrants: Patterns of Filipino, Korean, and Chinese Settlement in the United States. New York: Praeger.

Markowitz, Fran
1988a "Jewish in the USSR, Russian in the USA" Pp. 79-95. in Persistence and Flexibility: Anthropological Perspectives on the American Jewish Experience edited by Walter P. Zenner. Albany: SUNY Press.

_____
1988b "Rituals as Keys to Soviet Immigrants' Jewish Identity" Pp. 128-147 in Between Two Worlds: Ethnographic Essays on American Jewry edited by Jack Kugelmass. Ithaca: Cornell University Press.

_____
1990 "Responding to Events From Afar: Soviet Jewish Refugees Reassess Their Identity. Presentation for the Annual Meeting of the American Anthropological Association, New Orleans, November.

_____
1991 "The Not Lost Generation: Family Dynamics and Ethnic Identity Among Soviet Adolescent Immigrants if the 1970s" Paper presented at the Wilstein Institute for Jewish Policy Studies Conference, Soviet Jewish Acculturation -- Beyond Resettlement, Palo Alto

_____
1992 "Community Without Organizations." City and Society 6 (2): 141-155.

_____
1993 A Community in Spite of Itself: Soviet Jewish Emigres in New York. Washington, D.C.: Smithsonian

_____
1994a "Family Dynamics and the Teenage Immigrant: Creating the Self Through the Parents' Image" Adolescence 29 (113): 151-61.

1994b "Soviet Dis-Union and the Fragmentation of Self: Implications for the Emigrating Jewish Family" East European Jewish Affairs 24(1):3-17

Martin, David R. and Susan Gibbs
1990 "Soviet Refugees: The Continuing Dilemma." GAO Journal, (Summer): 24-28.

Min, Pyong-Gap
1988 Ethnic Business Enterprise: Korean Small Business in Atlanta. Staten Island: Center for Migration Studies.

Murray, Michael and Associates
1981 A Report on Refugee Services in San Francisco. San Francisco: Center for Southeast Asian Refugee Resettlement
——— ed.
Asian Americans: Contemporary Trends and Issues. Newbury Park, Ca: Sage, 1994

Nagel, Joane
1986 "The Political Construction of Ethnicity." Pp. 93-112 in Competitive Ethnic Relations, edited by Susan Olzak and Joane Nagel. Orlando: Academic Press, Inc.

Nagel, Joane and Susan Olzak
1982 "Ethnic Mobilization in New and Old States: An Extension of the Competition Model." Social Problems 30 (2):127-143.

Navrozov, Lev
1994 "Zhirinovsky" Midstream (May):10-14.

New York Times
1989 "Visa Applicants Deluge Embassy in Moscow" (October 3) p. 4

Nezer, Zvi
1985 "The Emigration of Soviet Jews." Soviet Jewish Affairs 15(1):17-30.

Nielsen, Francois
1985 "Towards a Theory of Ethnic Solidarity in Modern Societies." American Sociological Review 50 (2): 133-149.

Noonan, Leo
1988 "Russians Go Republican." The Jewish Journal, November 18-24: 31.

Orbach, Alexander
1980 "The Jewish of Soviet-Jewish Culture: Historical Considerations." Journal of Jewish Communal Service LVII (3): 145-153.

Orleck, Annalise
1987 "The Soviet Jews: Life in Brighton Beach, Brooklyn" pp. 273-304. in New Immigrants in New York, edited by Nancy Foner. New York: Columbia University Press.

ORR (Office of Refugee Resettlement)
1982   Report to Congress: Refugee Resettlement Program. Washington, D.C.: Office of Refugee Resettlement

———   1983   Report to Congress: Refugee Resettlement Program. Washington, D.C.: Office of Refugee Resettlement

———   1984   Report to Congress: Refugee Resettlement Program. Washington, D.C.: Office of Refugee Resettlement

———   1988   Report to Congress: Refugee Resettlement Program. Washington, D.C.: Office of Refugee Resettlement

———   1989   Report to Congress: Refugee Resettlement Program. Washington, D.C.: Office of Refugee Resettlement

———   1990   Report to Congress: Refugee Resettlement Program. Washington, D.C.: Office of Refugee Resettlement

———   1991   Report to Congress: Refugee Resettlement Program. Washington, D.C.: Office of Refugee Resettlement

———   1992   Report to Congress: Refugee Resettlement Program. Washington, D.C.: Office of Refugee Resettlement

———   1993   Report to Congress: Refugee Resettlement Program. Washington, D.C.: Office of Refugee Resettlement

Panish, Paul
1981   Exit Visa. New York: McCann and Geoghegan.

Paretzky, Harvey
1993a An Employment Profile of Soviet Jewish Refugees in the United States. New York: Council of Jewish Federations. (Mimeo)

Parlin, Bradley
1976   Immigrant Professionals in the United States. New York: Praeger.

Pfefferman, Naomi
1989   "The Viennese Connection." The Jewish Journal, February 10-16: 18.

Pinkus, Benjamin
1985   "National Identity and Emigration Patterns Among Soviet Jewry." Soviet Jewish Affairs 15 (3): 3-27.

Piore, Michael J.
1979   Birds of Passage. New York: Cambridge University Press

_____
1986 "The Shifting Grounds for Immigration." The Annals 485. (May):23-33.

Portes, Alejandro and Robert Bach
1985 Latin Journey: Cuban and Mexican Immigrants in the United States. Berkeley: University of California Press.

Portes, Alejandro and Robert D. Manning
1986 "The Immigrant Enclave: Theory and Empirical Examples." Pp. 47-68 in Competitive Ethnic Relations, edited by Susan Olzak and Joane Nagel. Orlando: Academic Press, Inc.

Portes, Alejandro and Ruben Rumbaut
1990 Immigrant America: A Portrait. Berkeley: University of California Press.

Razin, Eran
1990 "Immigrant Entrepreneurs in Israeli, Canada and California" UCLA ISSR Working Papers in the Social Sciences Vol 5, No. 8

Reimers, David M.
1985 Still the Golden Door: The Third World Comes to America. New York: Columbia University Press.

Rischin, Moses
1962 The Promised City. Cambridge: Harvard University Press.

Rose, Peter I. (ed.)
1986 Working with Refugees. New York: Center for Migration Studies.

Rosner, Lydia
1986 The Soviet Way of Crime: Beating the System in the Soviet Union and the U.S.A. South Hadley, Massachusetts: Bergin and Garvey.

Ruby, Walter
1993 "Russian Jews in America" Jewish World, April 2-8 pp. 16-19.

Rueschemeyer, Marilyn, Igor Golomshtok and Janet Kennedy
1985 Soviet Emigre Artists: Life and Work in the USSR and the United States. Armonk, New York: M.E. Sharpe.

Russell, Raymond
1985 Sharing Ownership in the Workplace. Albany: SUNY Press.

Russian Language Telephone Directory
1991 Los Angeles: Almanac Enterprises Inc

Schiff, Alvin I.
1980 "Language, Culture and the Jewish Acculturation of Soviet Jewish Emigres." Journal of Jewish Communal Service 57: (1):44-49.

Schneller, Debora Podolsky
  1981 "The Immigrant's Challenge: Mourning the Loss of Homeland and Adapting to the New World" Smith College Studies in Social Work LI(2):95-125.

Schwartz, Larry R.
  1980 "Soviet Jewish Resettlement: Operationalizing Jewish Consciousness Raising." Journal of Jewish Communal Service 57 (1):50-55.

Serels, M. Mitchell
  1990 "The Soviet Sephardim in the United States" New York: Yeshiva University. Mimeo.

Shlapentokh, Vladimir
  1984 Love, Marriage, and Friendship in the Soviet Union: Ideals and Practices. New York: Praeger.

Silverman, Myrna
  1988 "Family, Kinship and Ethnicity: Strategies for Social Mobility." Pp. 165-182. in Persistence and Flexibility: Anthropological Perspectives on the American Jewish Experience edited by Walter P. Zenner. Albany: SUNY Press.

Simon, Julian L.
  1986 "Basic Data Concerning Immigration to the United States" The Annals 487: 12-56.

Simon, Rita J. and Melanie Brooks
  1983 "Soviet Jewish Immigrants' Adjustment in Four United States Cities." Journal of Jewish Communal Service 60 (1): 56-64.

Simon, Rita J., ed.
  1983 "Refugee Families' Adjustment and Aspirations: A Comparison of Soviet Jewish and Vietnamese Immigrants." Ethnic and Racial Studies 6(4): 492-504.

  _____
  1985a New Lives: The Adjustment of Soviet Jewish Immigrants in the United States and Israel. Lexington, Massachusetts: Lexington Books.

  _____
  1985b Soviet Jews pp. 181-193 in David W. Haines (ed.) Refugees in the United States. Westport, CT: Greenwood Press.

Simon, Rita J. and Julian Simon
  1985 "Social and Economic Adjustment." in Rita J. Simon (ed.) New Lives: The Adjustment of Soviet Jewish Immigrants in the U.S. and Israel. Lexington, MA: Lexington Books.

Simon, Rita J., Julian Simon and Jim Schwartz
  1982 "The Soviet Jews Adjustment to the United States." Council of Jewish Federations.

Simon, Rita J. Louise Shelly and Paul Schneiderman
1986 "Social and Economic Adjustment of Soviet Jewish Women in the United States" pp. 76-94 in Rita James Simon and Caroline B. Brettell (eds.) International Migration: The Female Experience. Totowa, N.J.: Rowman and Allanheld.

Sluzki, Carlos E.
1979 "Migration and Family Conflict" Family Process 18 (4): 381-394.

Statistical Yearbook of the USSR
1979 Moscow.

Statistical Abstract of the United States
1984 Washington, DC.

Stutz, Rochelle P.
1984 Resettling Soviet Emigres: How Caseworkers Coped" Social Work (March-April): 187-188

Tenenbaum, Shelly
1993 A Credit to Their Community. Detroit: Wayne State University Press

Terlitsky, Leonard
1992 "Developing the Community of Jewish New Americans from the USSR in New York City" pp. 13-16 in Madeleine Tress and Deborah Bernick (editors) New Voices: The Integration of Soviet Emigres and Their Organizations Into the Jewish Communal World. New York: Council of Jewish Federations.

Tomakhin, G. D.
1980 Across the United States of America. Moscow: Prosveshcheniye

Tress, Madeleine
1991 "United States Policy Toward Soviet Emigration" Migration 3/4 (11/12):93-106

——
1994 Research Note: The Soviet-Jewish Refugee Populations in Germany and the United States Compared. New York: HIAS (MARCH)

Tress, Madeleine and Deborah Bernick
1992 New Voices: The Integration of Soviet Emigres and Their Organizations Into the Jewish Communal World. New York: Council of Jewish Federations.

Ungar, Sanford J.
1989 "Freedom's Door Shut in Face of Soviet Jews." Los Angeles Times. November 12: M2, M8.

UJA-Federation of New York
1995 "To be a Jew in the Ukraine is Not Easy" New York Times Magazine (April 30): 51

United States Bureau of the Census
   1983   1980 Census of Population, Detailed Population Characteris-
          tics, Part 6, California Section 1.
United States Bureau of the Census
   1993   1990 Census of Population
United States Immigration and Naturalization Service
   1993   Statistical Yearbook of the Immigration and Naturalization Ser-
          vice. Washington, DC: Department of Justice
Washington Processing Center ND (Instructions for application for refugee status).
Waxman, Chaim
   1990   "Is the Cup Half-Full or Half-Empty?: Perspectives on the Fu-
          ture of the American Jewish Community." Pp. 71-85 in Ameri-
          can Pluralism and the Jewish Community, edited by Seymour
          Martin Lipset. New Brunswick, N.J. Transaction.
Wirth, Louis
   1928   The Ghetto Chicago: University of Chicago Press.
Woo, Elaine
   1989   "Anticipated Reunion Turns Into a Nightmare for Soviet Emi-
          gre" Los Angeles Times. November 24. B1, B12.
Zahler, Gayle
   1989   Jewish Identity and the Soviet Emigre Newcomer. Paper Pre-
          sented at the National Conference of Jewish Communal Work-
          ers: Boca Raton, Florida. Zenner, Walter P. 1983 "The Jewish
          Diaspora and the Middleman Adaptation." Pp. 142-155 in Di-
          aspora: Exile and the Jewish Condition, edited by E. Levine.
          New York: Jason Aronson.

9 780205 167029

ISBN 0-205-16702-0

H67028